# BEST IN CLASS

## How We Closed the 5 Gaps™ of Academic Achievement

*Eric Y. Mahmoud, with Jeffrey A. Hassan*

*Papyrus Publishing Inc.*
*Brooklyn Park, Minnesota*

*Best in Class: How We Closed the 5 Gaps™ of Academic Achievement*
ISBN-13: 978-0-9882883-1-7 Softcover
ISBN-13: 978-0-9882883-2-4 Hardcover

Cover Photo by Knutson Photography, Inc.

Papyrus Publishing Inc.
Brooklyn Park, Minnesota, United States of America
PapyrusPublishing@msn.com

A portion of the proceeds from the sale of this book will be donated to Harvest Prep, Best Academy, and Mastery School.

# Dedication

This book is dedicated to the two most important women in my life. First, and foremost, my mother, Annie McLaughlin. My mother is the most caring, loving, compassionate, hardworking, and beautiful woman that I have known. My mother, through her example, taught me the importance of love and service to others.

She worked hard all of her life, especially for my three siblings and me. One of my most vivid memories of my mother was when I was 10 years old. On one cold, Christmas Eve night, she was late arriving home. She didn't have a car so I knew she had to take public transportation. She was out making sure that she got Christmas gifts for everyone – not only in our immediate family, but also for every family member's family. The Philadelphia West Oak Lane neighborhood where we lived was at times dangerous. Robberies and purse snatchings were regular occurrences. That night I was worried that she was coming home with an arm full of gifts in the middle of the night. After having worried late into the evening, I remember how relieved and happy I was to see her walk through the door that night. I thanked God and Santa that night for the greatest Christmas present ever - the safe return home of my momma!

My mother taught me both the joy and complexity of parenting. She attended every one of my parent-teacher conferences and sporting events. At one of my football games, in one of the tougher parts of the city, she even tried to break up a fight of over 50 teenage boys! There she was, in the midst of an all-out brawl, with boys cursing and fighting. Through it all, I could hear my mother's sweet voice saying, "Boys now stop fighting! You shouldn't be fighting!" I remember thinking to myself, 'My mom must be crazy if she thinks that these boys are going to listen to her and stop fighting.' I was able to grab her and swiftly sweep her off the field to safety. Thank you, Mom, for all that you've done for me!

Last, but by no means least, this book is dedicated to the seed that produced the Seed - my brilliant and beautiful wife, Dr. Ella Mahmoud. Although I get a lot of credit for the recent success of our schools, it is Ella that is truly the "wind beneath my wings." She is the founder of our schools, and all of this work that we've done over the past 30 years is a direct result of her incredible journey and her vision and love for children.

Along this incredible, stressful, and at times, uncertain, wonderful journey of developing our schools, she has been a rock of stability and support. I thank God for her vision and strength to withstand the "roller coaster ride" of success, failure, and then success again. Making history, pushing boundaries, and doing things that have never been done before can be an exhilarating, scary, and, at times, painful experience. It is not for the "faint of heart." It is only for those that are committed and who have been forged in the fire of controversy and shaped in the crucible of challenge. Ella Mahmoud has been forged and shaped in that crucible into the diamond of a woman that she is today. I'm honored and proud to be her husband.

# Acknowledgements

The list of people that I could thank for making this book possible would be very, very long, so forgive me if I fail to mention anyone specifically by name. I want to begin by giving thanks to God for providing me with the desire, passion, commitment, energy, and skill to serve my community. I thank God for entrusting me with the enormous responsibility of impacting the lives of so many wonderful children.

I want to thank my friend, attorney, and co-author of this book, Jeff Hassan. Jeff is a husband, father, lawyer, community activist, mentor to many students, and a great brother. The best word I can find that would describe Jeff would be "execution." The definition of execution is getting things done. For the almost 30 years that I've known Jeff Hassan, he's always exhibited the incredible and unique ability to get things done. Whether it's starting up a new school like our Mastery School, managing a two-million-dollar building renovation in a low-income neighborhood, winning a police misconduct court case, to completing a book, you can count on Jeff to get things done.

About four years ago Jeff said to me, "Brother, you need to write a book." I acknowledged that it was a good idea, but thought to myself, 'When would I have the time to do it?' For the next two years Jeff would encourage/harass me to start writing a book about my experience in education. Each time I would acknowledge that, yes, I should write it, but, again, when would I find the time.

Finally, two years ago, Jeff said to me, "Look, man, I'll write the darn book. We've got to get this done!" Once again, I thought to myself that this was a great idea and a generous offer, but I was still concerned about the time commitment it would take. After all, I was overseeing the operation of five schools for more than 1,200 children. Just to keep him off my back, for the next year-and-a-half, we started meeting at his house just about every Sunday morning, where I would dictate and he would write. He even harassed me into taking three days during spring break to leave town and sequester ourselves as we were nearing completion. Thank God we finally got it done. Completing this book would not have been possible if it were not for Jeff's persistence, guidance, excellent writing ability, but most importantly, his skill in executing. Thank you so much, Jeff, for making the dream of writing this book a reality.

I would also like to thank a few others that made this book possible:

Kim Nelson, Vice President of General Mills, heard me give a presentation on my "5 Gaps" analysis of the achievement gap. As the head of one of the General Mills marketing divisions, she instinctively knew that I had hit upon something with the "5 Gaps" analysis. And, as the co-chair of the Education Work Group of the African-American Leadership Forum (AALF), she encouraged AALF to use the "5 Gaps" analysis as the hallmark of its 2011 publication, *A Crisis in Our Community*, and as the organizing framework for addressing solutions to the achievement gap. As a result of her recognition, the "5 Gaps" framework of analysis has now become a part of the Minnesota education reform movement's lexicon. This was another motivation to write the book.

I also want to acknowledge Louis King for his support over the years as we developed our schools. Louis is CEO of Summit Academy Opportunities Industrialization Center, and a friend and parent of a 6th grade scholar that attends Harvest Preparatory School. He has acted in many other capacities in support of our institutions. His advice over the many years I have known him has been invaluable.

I want to give a very special thank you to Dr. Callie Lalugba, Chief Academic Officer for Harvest Prep, Best Academy, and Mastery School. She has provided the educational leadership for our schools for the past 11 years. I have often said that she is one on the best principals in the state of Minnesota; and that is now evident to anyone who knows our schools. She has been instrumental in leading our schools to the greatest academic gains for African-American and other low-income children in the history of Minnesota. Her drive, determination, and sheer will has catapulted our schools into the state and national spotlight as a direct result of her instructional leadership.

I also want to thank Dr. Bernadeia Johnson, Superintendent of Minneapolis Public Schools. She had the bold vision and leadership to be there for me and our schools at a time when it was not popular for a public school district to help a charter school. She was the bold architect of the vision to enter into a groundbreaking partnership between Minneapolis Public Schools and the leadership of our network of schools to establish four new Mastery Schools - a partnership model that is scheduled to be the focus of a CNN news network broadcast in 2013. It is our hope and desire that this partnership becomes a national model for what is possible when we put the education of children first, before the consideration of adults.

I want to thank Rev. Dr. Alphonse Reff, Sr., and Wayman AME Church (Wayman) for their incredible partnership with our schools. Wayman donated land, which allowed Harvest Prep and Best Academy to build an addition to our building. This has given our schools the added capacity to educate hundreds of additional children every year. Rev. Dr. Reff and the Wayman congregation understood the impact that a quality education would have on our community. The contribution of their land, free of charge, to help expand our schools has been one the most forward thinking, selfless acts that I have ever encountered. I thank God for Rev. Dr. Reff and the Wayman congregation for all that they've done for our community.

A personal thank you goes to the board chairs of each of our schools. All of them bring tremendous skill, expertise, and commitment to their roles. Ezra Hyland, Teaching Specialist in the

University of Minnesota's Department of Postsecondary Teaching and Learning, is the board chair of Best Academy; Shana Ford, Branch Manager and Vice President at BMO Harris Bank, is the board chair of Harvest Prep; and Sylvia Bartley, a Ph.D. in Neurophysiology who trains brain surgeons from around the world on deep brain stimulation surgery for Medtronic, Inc., is the board chair of the new Mastery School.

I would be remiss if I did not mention the tremendous financial support that our schools receive from various philanthropic organizations that have allowed us to achieve our success. The Robins, Kaplan, Miller & Ciresi Foundation, under the leadership of Mike Ciresi, has been a strong supporter of our schools, providing funding for professional development of our teaching staff, helping bridge the budget gap when the state delayed funding of K-12 education between 2010 and 2012. The I.A. O'Shaughnessy Foundation has provided tremendous support for Best Academy and is hugely responsible for the success Best has achieved over the past three years in closing the gap, particularly for boys. General Mills has been a longtime supporter and staunch backer of the mission at Harvest Prep, Best Academy, and now in providing significant start-up funding for the new Mastery School. Cargill Foundation has provided both academic and operational support through its program called Lead for Charter Schools. Target Foundation is a leader in support of K-12 education in Minnesota, and has been an incredible partner in our mission. They funded the complete makeover of the schools' library and provided computer workstations for the children. They provide literacy support for students and professional development training for teachers; and every month they provide food support for our families through their Meals for Minds program through Second Harvest Heartland. Thomson Reuters and Boston Scientific have provided mentoring support to our students that have allowed us to close the achievement gap.

Finally, I want to thank the parents, staff, board of directors, and supporters of Harvest Preparatory School, Seed Academy, Best Academy, Sister Academy, Best Academy East, and Mastery School for all of your hard work, dedication, and trust that you have placed in me and the mission of our schools. There are too many names to mention that have played a role over the past 25 years; but please know that I love all of you and appreciate what you have done in making the successes of our schools a reality. This book would not be possible if it were not for what you've collectively produced – a national school model!

# Contents

# PREFACE

After reading many books over the years regarding the achievement gap between White children and children of color, Eric Mahmoud observed that very few were solution oriented; most simply admired the problem. After 25 years of experience in educating children of color and having some success, he thought it important to share that success with other educators, policymakers and the public.

Eric Mahmoud came to the education arena with the idea that education was the lever for community development. Originally, he thought that economic development was the key to community development, and that he would use his background in engineering to develop industry and manufacturing in the African-American community as a means of addressing the social conditions faced in our community. His goal, as early as a teenager, had been to start a manufacturing plant in his Philadelphia, Pennsylvania neighborhood of West Oak Lane.

His wife, Dr. Ella Mahmoud, was the first to introduce him to the importance of education. After watching and supporting her in the development of her preschool program of Seed Academy, it became clear to him that education, not economic development, was the lever that had the transformative power to change the people's lives.

In 1983, after having graduated from the University of Wisconsin with a degree in engineering, and having worked with Honeywell, Medtronic, and African-American-owned Juno Enterprises, he quit his "good job" as an engineer to become the first principal of the K-6 Harvest Preparatory School. Through a lot of trial and error, research, and hard work, he and his wife developed two of the most successful K-8 public educational institutions in the state of Minnesota and, indeed, the country.

For the first 13 years of their effort, Harvest Preparatory School (Harvest Prep) could brag about being the "Best of the Worst" – meaning they were outperforming all of the other public schools in Minnesota in educating low-income children of color in math and reading, but were still well below the Minnesota state average. However, between 2005 and 2008 a major sea change occurred. First, in 2005, Eric suffered a ruptured appendix, which required emergency surgery. During surgery it was discovered that he had a cancerous cyst on his colon, which, had it not been discovered, would have eventually metastasized and led to his death. This caused him to take a serious look at what he was doing in his life and at their school, and make a commitment to himself that Harvest Prep would become the "Best of the Best." In 2008 the election of Barack Obama, the first African-American president in the history of the United States, forever changed the narrative for what was possible and helped him to galvanize the idea of becoming the "Best of the Best." His goal from that point on was to create as many Barack and Michelle Obamas as humanly possible. He set about his vision with a missionary zeal, by visiting, researching, and studying as many high-performing public schools for low-income children as he could find. Over the next five years, from 2008 to 2013, he restructured and retooled their program to move to the next level.

Also, in 2008, he discovered that the boys at their school, who were primarily African-American, were a full grade level behind their girls; and it became apparent to him that their condition required special attention. Consequently, that year Best Academy was created to focus on the special needs of boys. Beginning in 2008, the boys went from the 50th and 60th percentiles in math and reading on state standardized testing, to the 80th percentile in both math and reading in 2012, surpassing the statewide average in each category.

In 2012 and 2013, Harvest Prep and Best Academy were the recipients of state and national awards for "Beating the Odds" with low-income children of color. In 2012 Eric Mahmoud and his team of teachers and administrators were invited to enter into a partnership with Minneapolis Public Schools to start four new "Mastery Schools" over the next 10 years to expand educational opportunities to low-income and socially-disadvantaged children in the city of Minneapolis. This public school/charter school collaborative between the leaders of Harvest Prep, Best Academy, and Minneapolis Public Schools piqued the interest of CNN broadcast journalist Soledad O'Brien for her series *Black in America*. CNN followed and filmed the development of the first Mastery School that began in 2012, and the success of Harvest Prep and Best Academy. It is anticipated that the program will air in some time in 2013, corresponding with the release of this book.

That brings us to the writing of this book. After being asked, encouraged, and then finally harangued into writing about his schools' success, he finally agreed that it was sufficiently important to put his thoughts and ideas into the public space. Beginning with the publication of *A Crisis in Our Community*, produced by the African-American Leadership Forum here in Minneapolis, Eric introduced his thesis of the "5 Gaps" in Black/White educational achievement. The premise of his thesis is that the so-called achievement gap is not just one amorphous gap; but is a combination of five gaps. Those five gaps, which are discussed in detail in Chapter 5 of this book, are the Preparation, Time, Leadership, Teacher, and Belief gaps.

It is Eric's hope and desire that this book serves as an inspiration for what is possible in educating poor and socially-disadvantaged children of color. His premise is, "The challenge of educating Black children is not a hardware problem, but rather a software problem. There's nothing wrong with the hardware (i.e. the intellectual capacity of the children); the problem is that the wrong software is being used to program them for success." When the adults make up their minds and organize themselves for the success of children, there are no limits to what all children can accomplish – regardless of their social, economic, or family circumstances.

This book is organized in several stages, moving from the general to the specific. It begins with the story of Eric and his wife founding Harvest Prep and Best Academy, and their personal histories and backgrounds. Chapter 2 discusses the Social Costs associated with the educational achievement gap. The next two chapters, 3 and 4, tell the story of the founding of the two schools; and the fifth chapter, the "5 Gaps" Framework of Analysis, begins his analysis of and solution to the Black/White educational achievement gap. The final two chapters, 6 and 7, are primarily for educational practitioners who want to know "How We Get it Done." People are always asking him, "What do you do that is different?" Chapter 6 sets forth the formula that he and his team have used at his schools in closing the achievement gap, and Chapter 7 provides a set of "10 Best Practices" employed by leaders of several of the gap-closing schools in the Minneapolis-St. Paul metro area.

At the beginning of each chapter is a vignette about a student who has attended Harvest Prep or Best. While the names have been changed, the events are true. And while the vignettes describe individual students, they reflect the challenges faced by many students attending our urban schools. Not only do these vignettes describe the challenges faced by students, parents and schools, they also describe the tremendous success achieved and the satisfaction received from seeing children overcome obstacles.

Please note that throughout the book when comparing the differences between two percentages, the most common analysis is to subtract the two percentages to determine the percentage-point difference. The authors have chosen to analyze the differences between two percentages as a "percentage of the percentage." For example on page 57 the graph shows the difference between Harvest math 81% proficiency and the state math 62% proficiency in 2012 was a 19 percentile-point difference. The actual percentage difference is 31%. This conclusion is derived by subtracting 62% from 81% and then dividing by 62% ( (81-62)/62) = 30.6.

One final word that should be added: In writing this book the authors are aware that the notion of a so-called "achievement gap" is rife with racial implications. The implicit suggestion that there is an "achievement gap" because of racial differences feeds into the belief that there are differences in human intelligence based upon one's racial identity. That is why many African-American and other educators reject the notion of an "achievement gap," and instead prefer to refer to it as an "opportunity gap." The term "achievement gap" is used in this book as a starting point for a common frame of reference. The authors hope that those who are sensitive to the use of this terminology will bear with them, and understand that the goal is to move us from where we are to where we need to be.

# Introduction

"Beginning with the end in mind" is a phrase coined by Stephen R. Covey, author of *7 Habits of Highly Effective People*. It means that before one sets out to accomplish a task, s/he should first have a clear understanding of the desired outcome in mind, and then work backwards from there.

This book begins with the desired outcome in mind of demonstrating what is possible for a group of children who, because of race, economic status, or zip code, our school systems have failed; a group of children for whom many people believe that academic success is impossible.

2013 Sister Academy 8th grade valedictorian Asante Samuels embodies the desired outcome for the students that attend the schools discussed in this book - Harvest Preparatory School, Best Academy, Sister Academy, Best East, and Mastery School. Asante's graduation speech, entitled "The Magic of Intelligence," tells the story of what is possible in educating our children.

## The Magic of Intelligence

*"Good morning! I'm Asante Samuels and I'd like to begin my speech with a story of sorts. There was a girl, about 2 years ago, who didn't understand what Albert Einstein was able to put so clearly, and that was, "The sign of true intelligence is not knowledge, but imagination." You see, the girl was trapped in a dream, and dreams are fine, as long as you can wake up. She refused to accept reality and saw her imagination as simply another useless nothing. The world was boring; imagination could not help you here because there was no... magic. And she knew this because she had checked her closet several times. Until one day when the girl discovered magic in the one place she had never thought to look; in the one*

*place that in the past, she would have rejected - school. Now, who would've thought that the reality she hid from would save her. She found magic in this place; it became a castle in which she learned that her imagination could expand possibilities if she utilized it to push her knowledge. She'd been locked in her imagination so long she didn't realize that in the real world, imagination is the equation for intelligence. Harvest Prep made me love that girl. That girl I was so ashamed of. That girl was me.*

*You see Harvest Prep has a magic that I have witnessed change lives, and magical people who've changed mine. And for that, I would like to thank Ms. Benkusky, Dr. Clarkson, my mentor Ms. Skelton, and all my teachers and coaches for saving my education and believing in me. Dr. and Mr. Mahmoud for founding this school and giving me the chance to remake myself, and take control of my future, my family who may or may not be superheroes, for everything, and my classmates, for challenging me.*

*This fall I'll be going to DeLaSalle High School where I plan to graduate with honors, and then to Brown University to get my PhD in the Earth Sciences. But, without my classmates, I would have thought none of this possible. You've all taught me so much. Never shall I forget the importance of sitting in the same bus seat, every day, or your language that is Zanguage. Nor shall I forget the brilliant smiles, the unity, and the fierce personalities. I love all of you. As we go into this new phase of our lives, I hope all of us discover the magic we hold. Though I was only here a short time, I'm happy it was with all of you. Always remember you are powerful. We are at the point in our lives that defines our future. Take control of it, conquer your challenges, and believe in your intelligence! Believe in your magic, and most of all, believe in yourself."*

Closing the achievement gap is not rocket science; it's harder than that! We've been able to figure out how to send a rocket to the moon, Mars, and beyond; but we still haven't been able to figure out how to close the Black/White achievement gap in the United States.

While the state of Minnesota, where this story takes place, is heralded nationally for its academic achievement of school-age children, student test scores in Minnesota have been stagnant in reading, declining in math, and abysmal in science over the past several years. While the city of Minneapolis is the context in which this particular story occurs, the demographics and other statistics relative to African-American school-age children and their academic performance in school could be transposed to virtually any urban area in America.

If Minnesota has historically been seen as a national oasis of academic achievement, it pales in comparison to the academic performance of other countries. Praising Minnesota test scores nationally is damning with faint praise because out of 34 so-called developed countries around the world, the United States ranked 14th in reading, 17th in science, and 25th in math in 2009.[1] Even though 2009 U.S. test scores were all higher than comparable scores from 2003 and 2006, they were still far behind the highest scoring countries like South Korea, Finland, Singapore, Hong Kong and Shanghai in China, and Canada.[2]

Within the U.S. educational system, African-American students are the canary in the coal mine. African-American and Native American students rank at or near the bottom of every major educational statistical category in math, reading, and science.

In Minnesota, the achievement gap for African-American students is even more egregious than the national average. While White students in Minnesota consistently rank in the top 10-15% nationally in academic performance, African-American students in Minnesota rank at or near the bottom. African-American students in Minnesota fare worse than African-American students in almost every other state. Minnesota has one of the highest educational disparities between White and Black students in the entire country. According to information released in January 2011 by the Minnesota Campaign for Achievement Now (MinnCAN), analysis of Minnesota's National Assessment of Education Progress test scores show that African-American students in fourth grade in Minnesota score worse in reading than African-American students in Alabama and Kentucky, with only 12% proficiency. That means that 88% are not proficient in reading. By the eighth grade the black/white achievement gap was the 2nd worst in the country in math, and 3rd worst in the country in reading.[3]

As Figure 1 illustrates, the achievement gap in Minnesota is not just an urban problem in low-income schools, where White students' math scores in Minneapolis and St. Paul are around 200% higher than Black students' scores; the gap affects upper-income suburban school districts as well, where White math scores are 75-90% higher than Black.[149]

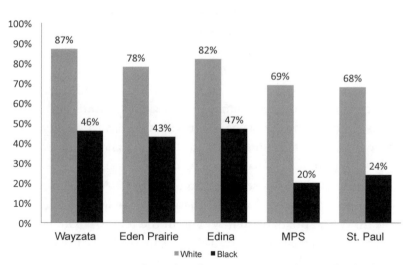

**Minnesota's Math Achievement Gap**
**Urban and Suburban School Districts**

Figure 1. Minnesota's Math Achievement Gap Urban and Suburban School Districts, 2012.

The reason for these differences is not what some might presume—racial differences somehow make White students smarter than African-American students. Consider the fact that the 1,200 African-American students attending the two gap-closing schools discussed in this book, Harvest Prep and Best Academy, score 19-20% higher in math than White students in Minneapolis and St. Paul, and they score either equal to or higher than every upper-income suburban school district in the Minneapolis metro area with the exception of Wayzata.[149] That's why Harvest Prep and Best are referred to as myth busters. As Eric Mahmoud, cofounder of Harvest Prep and Best Academy points out, *"The challenge of educating Black children is not a hardware problem, but rather a software problem. There's nothing wrong with the hardware (i.e. the intellectual capacity of the children); the problem is the wrong software is being used to program them for success."*

The No Child Left Behind law passed by Congress in 2001, and Title I of the Elementary and Secondary Education Act (1965) were specifically designed to narrow class and racial gaps in school performance by creating common expectations for all. Title I provides funding to states that develop plans to close the achievement gap for socially and economically disadvantaged students, and NCLB requires schools and districts to focus their attention on the academic achievement of traditionally underserved groups of children, such as low-income students, and students of major racial and ethnic subgroups.

The focus on the achievement gap in Minnesota has become a matter of grave importance and the subject of myriad efforts. According to Julie Sweitzer, Director of Leadership Initiatives for the College Readiness Consortium at the University of Minnesota, in 2011, there were more than 500 separate programs and initiatives in Minnesota alone designed to address the achievement gap. And according to a recent 2012 analysis by philanthropic organizations in

Minnesota, more than 90 million dollars is spent annually on various gap-closing initiatives – none of which have been particularly successful to date!

The lack of educational attainment by African-American children is associated with significant social costs. Education is directly correlated to income and wealth, and the lack of education is directly correlated to higher rates of crime and incarceration, higher rates of unemployment, higher rates of health disparities, and higher rates of poverty. North Minneapolis, where Harvest Prep and Best Academy are located, has become the epicenter of Minnesota's educational achievement gap between African-American and White students. In Minneapolis Public Schools (MPS) intense focus has been placed on the underperforming schools in north Minneapolis.

While some well-meaning, but uninformed, people question why north Minneapolis has become the subject of such intense focus, the answer is simple: north Minneapolis has the largest concentration of African-Americans in Minnesota. It has the lowest high school graduation rates, the highest rate of violent crime, the highest rate of unemployment, the lowest rate of home ownership, and some of the highest health disparities of any community in the state of Minnesota. The child poverty rate for African-American children in Minneapolis is a whopping 61%, compared to 8% of White children.[4] In north Minneapolis, the disparity is even greater. Homicide in north Minneapolis is almost one-half (48%) of the city's total homicide rate, even though it has less than one-fifth (18%) of the city's population. For young African-Americans, homicide is the leading cause of death in north Minneapolis. In one sector of north Minneapolis where the Northside Achievement Zone (NAZ)[5] is located, 25% of the students are either homeless or highly mobile—another factor that is highly correlated with low academic achievement. Home foreclosures in that same NAZ sector were four times as high as the city average, and vacant or condemned homes were almost nine times the population rate for that area. Teen pregnancy rates are twice as high in north

Minneapolis as the rest of the city, and 51% of families in north Minneapolis have single heads of households, primarily female —yet another factor correlated with lower academic achievement. If a solution to the educational achievement gap for African-American students can be found in north Minneapolis, it can be found anywhere. In the words of Eric Mahmoud, *"Finding a cure for closing the achievement gap is like discovering a cure for cancer."*

Finally, some people believe that focusing on closing the achievement gap for African-American children will somehow detract from the achievement of other students. But in a number of school districts just the opposite has occurred. Montgomery County, Maryland is an example, where significant strides have been made in closing the Black/White achievement gap. White student test scores have improved as the achievement gap between Black and White students was narrowed. Finding a cure for the lack of educational achievement among African-American students will not only benefit those students, but all students, whether white, brown, red, or yellow. Finding a solution for educating children in the most extreme circumstances, such as those in north Minneapolis, will go a long way towards curing what ails the rest of the Minnesota educational system, and could, indeed, serve as a model for the entire country. Just as curb cut ramps in sidewalks have benefited all pedestrians—those with handicaps, children, senior citizens and bicycle riders alike— finding a cure for the low academic achievement of African-American students will have far-reaching benefit for all students.

# 1

## The Founders

*Education is the passport to the future, for tomorrow belongs to those who prepare for it today.*
                                        *- El Hajj Malik Shabazz (aka Malcolm X)*

### Case Study 1: Dwight

Dwight is a living example of what closing the achievement gap means. Dwight, an 8th grade student, had been a special education student most of his school life, and began as a special education student at Best Academy, one of the schools discussed in this book. Best Academy has a boys-focused program as a part of its overall academic structure. Low expectations for African-American boys are pervasive in general education, and exceptionally low in special education, where they are justified, and more often than not, excused, by educators. Even Harvest Prep School and Best Academy, which take pride in overcoming stereotypes about what is possible, have had to fight the belief of low expectations for its special education students. Dwight is a living testament to what is possible.

Dwight had been a student at Harvest Prep and Best Academy for four years. Throughout this time he had displayed a very low level of motivation for academic achievement. While Dwight could memorize the words to all of the current hip hop music and was a video game master, he had very little interest in memorizing for any of his academic subjects. He spent at least half of the day in special education classes for reading and math. During Dwight's 8th grade year, the light came on. He decided that he no longer wanted the stigma associated with being a special education student that required him to leave his regular education class early to go to his special education class. Suddenly, he refused to go to special education classes any longer and made a conscious decision to compete with all students. His 8th grade reading teacher, who was new to the school and knew nothing about Dwight's history in special education, was focused on her professional goal of getting at least 80% of her students proficient in reading on the Minnesota Comprehensive Assessment (MCA) test by the end of the school year. With a significant amount of struggle, she exceeded even her own expectations: 100% of her 8th grade boys, including Dwight, achieved proficiency in reading on the 2011 MCA test. Dwight, who had never achieved anything higher than a D (Does Not Meet Standards) on previous MCA testing, achieved an E (Exceeds Standards)!

Two reasons were identified for Dwight's phenomenal results. First, he made up his mind that he no longer wanted to be labeled as a special education student. Secondly, Dwight's teacher was exceptionally gifted and knew how to teach critical thinking skills. Both student and teacher made a conscious decision to close the achievement gap.

This story of how the achievement gap was closed at Harvest Prep and Best Academy has to begin with the history of the founders of these two schools, Ella and Eric Mahmoud. Success does not occur in a vacuum, and is not without hard work. In order to understand the extraordinary effort that it takes to close the achievement gap one must understand the motivation and sense of urgency behind the effort.

## Ella Mahmoud

Ella's mother and father, Odessa and Gene Gates, moved to Minneapolis, Minnesota from Aberdeen, Mississippi, in 1969, when Ella was nine years old. Aberdeen is a small country town on the banks of the Tombigbee River in Monroe County, with a population of about 5,000. In the 1800s Aberdeen was one of Mississippi's largest ports for the cotton trade and, for a time, Mississippi's second largest city.

Ella Gates' parents moved to Minneapolis to find a better life for their children, away from the racial segregation, bigotry, and lack of opportunity for African-Americans in Mississippi in the late sixties and early seventies. Neither of Ella's parents could read or write, but, like most African-American parents at that time, they valued education for their children. Ella's father, who was a construction worker by day, had a variety of side jobs known as "hustles," which he worked in the evenings and on the weekends to make ends meet.

As a young child Ella was a stutterer, which caused her to produce sounds like "ca-ca-ca-can" and "llllike." The impact of stuttering on a person's functioning and emotional state can be severe. They may fear having to enunciate specific vowels or consonants and fear being caught stuttering in social situations; they experience self-imposed isolation, anxiety, stress, shame, or feel a "loss of control" during speech.

When Ella was growing up in the sixties and seventies, stuttering was thought to be a reflection of a child's lack of mental capacity or intelligence. As a result, she was placed in special education classes when she arrived at Horace Mann Elementary School in Minneapolis. Ella remembers that she and other special education students were labeled and stigmatized as being "dumb," although we know today that some of the world's greatest leaders, inventors, and actors—Winston Churchill, King George IV, Thomas Edison, and James Earl Jones—were stutterers.

Ella, along with the other special education children, was pulled out of her regular education classes each day to receive special tutoring for their perceived impairment. She remembers that one day each week she and the other special education students were loaded onto a "short bus" and shuttled off to another building where they received tutoring. But as Ella recalls, it was not with another human being, but with a typewriter-like machine. It would say a sentence, which she would then repeat. She thought it very strange to find herself in a room with only a machine to practice speech.

Although Ella was singled out and teased by other children for being dumb, she was blessed to have Mrs. Barbara Owens, a teacher who saw the potential in her to do great things in her life. Mrs. Owens was originally from the south herself, and Ella sensed the empathy that she had for her. Even as a nine-year-old child Ella sensed the caring that Mrs. Owens had. Mrs. Owens knew that Ella had some forces, like her dialect and southern/rural culture, working against her in her migration to a new and strange environment. Ella didn't have school supplies like other children and one day decided to use the rubber bottom on her shoe to erase something she had written on paper. Other students saw this and started laughing. Mrs. Owens walked over to Ella, put her hand on her shoulder and said loudly and clearly, so that everyone could hear, "Ella, that was a very good idea using your shoe as an eraser. The bottom is rubber, and rubber helps erase lead from paper." As Ella lifted her head from crying she saw other students using the bottom of their shoes to erase their mistakes, too.

Ella recalls, "My mother gave me life, but Mrs. Owens gave me a new lease on life." Mrs. Owen protected her as a mother duck protects her ducklings. Her hugs and assurances helped to soothe the negative comments that other teachers made about the funny way she and her parents talked. Mrs. Owens always encouraged Ella and told her she was not dumb, and that she had the same ability as all of the other children to realize her dreams. Ella still vividly remembers the day she left her field trip permission slip at home. In a panic she called her mother and asked her to please bring "my slip" to school so she could go on the field trip with the other children. When her mother arrived she was carrying a brown paper bag with Ella's slip—the garment she wore underneath her dress. Ella was devastated with embarrassment. But Mrs. Owens, who didn't blink an eye, got Mrs. Gates' approval on the form and sent Ella on her way.

From that day on Ella Mahmoud knew she wanted to help other children like herself. Instead of feeling defeated by the teasing she suffered as a special education student, she felt stronger. When Ella told her father she was being placed in special education classes and that the other kids at school were teasing her, her father built her a little schoolhouse attached to the garage in the alley behind the family home. Even though he couldn't read or write her father understood the importance and power of education for his daughter. In that little schoolhouse, Ella Gates taught her three brothers and countless other kids in the neighborhood, and encouraged them to value the importance of education.

Thus began Ella Gates' vision for what is now known as Seed Academy preschool, Harvest Preparatory School (Harvest Prep), and Best Academy (Best). Mrs. Owens' voice would remain in Ella's consciousness for the rest of her life. It is the voice of Mrs. Owens that continues to motivate her and inspire the work that she continues to do over 40 years later. Because of her own experiences Ella can recognize the same innate strengths, talents, and abilities in the children that she serves. She knows that those strengths, talents, and abilities have to be nurtured and developed.

Even in junior high school Ella continued to experience a repeat of some of the same shaming experiences from her teachers and fellow students. Being of dark complexion with kinky hair, and still carrying a southern accent, she was often teased because of her skin color, hair texture, and the way she talked. This reinforced her feeling of lack of worth and low self-esteem. As a result of her own negative experiences Ella learned to discern when a person working with children was genuinely interested and caring. By high school Ella was on a track to becoming an office secretary instead of being on a track to go to college. She observed that her guidance counselor at Central High School in Minneapolis directed some of her classmates to college level preparatory classes, which she was never offered. When she asked her counselor about taking college prep classes instead of sewing and typing she was told, "College is for students that have been prepared for it, and Ella, you haven't been prepared for it." The counselor went on to compliment Ella on her typing speed and sewing handiwork. Ella complained to her principal, Dr. Joyce Jackson, who happened to be African-American – one of only a handful of African-American principals in Minneapolis. Dr. Jackson immediately enrolled Ella in classes like Geometry, Trigonometry, Chemistry, and English Literature. Ella remembers being on an accelerated ride that at times was moving at a faster pace than she had been accustomed; but one that she greatly enjoyed. She passed every class and did well enough on her ACT and SAT exams to be accepted at the University of Wisconsin.

Ella matriculated to the University of Wisconsin in Madison in 1978, where she majored in Communications. During that freshman year she met Eric McLaughlin, and the following year, 1979, they started dating and continued until Ella left school after her junior year in 1981 to care for her ailing mother in Minneapolis. However, she continued with her education by taking classes at the University of Minnesota and finished her undergraduate degree in organizational management at Concordia University in St. Paul, Minnesota. Ella got work as a freelance reporter for the *Minneapolis Spokesman/St. Paul*

*Recorder* and assistant editor for the *Twin Cities Courier* – two local newspapers serving primarily the African-American community in Minneapolis and St. Paul.

After Eric graduated from the University of Wisconsin in 1983, he moved to Minneapolis to join Ella. The two married shortly thereafter, and in 1984 they adopted a two-year-old girl. At the same time they became foster parents and would later adopt the two foster children they were raising.

In 1985 Ella started a daycare in her home with four children – two infants and two preschool students. The decision to start a daycare was more pragmatic than idealistic: she wanted her newly-adopted baby daughter to be in a nurturing environment where she could be "molded correctly."

The following year, 1986, Ella attended the United Nations Decade for Women's World Conference in Nairobi, Kenya as a reporter for the Twin Cities Courier. Ella's sister-in-law and mother-in-law stayed with her daughter and the children in her daycare for the month that she was gone. The trip would serve to be a life-changing experience for her. At the conference Ella met African women from all over the world and was often mistaken for a Kenyan or a member of some other neighboring African tribe. This gave her a sense of pride, self-esteem, and awareness that she had not previously experienced; it helped her to identify with and to link her to her ancestral past.

At the conference she learned about women's issues from all over the world, including the custom of female circumcision (also known as female genital mutilation, which typically involves partial or total removal of the external genitalia) practiced in certain African and Middle Eastern cultures. What Ella found interesting is that the women who were a part of those cultures did not have a problem with it. It was the women from other parts of the world who thought the practice inhumane and barbaric that told the women that it was unacceptable. Ella found this paradoxical. Thirty years later Ella would witness a similar paradox, when she observed that parents and families of African-American children were satisfied with their children's teachers and schools, even though they were failing to educate their children.

Although she had long been inspired to help educate children, before her trip to Kenya Ella had not conceived the idea of starting a school. She had been content running her daycare and happy with her career as a freelance reporter and writer. But in Kenya she saw young girls wearing uniforms and holding hands walking to and from school. In their clean and neatly pressed uniforms, each bearing a Coat of Arms, she could not distinguish the poor child from the wealthy child. At first she thought it was odd that the girls were holding hands because she had never seen this before where she had lived. The big girls helped carry the smaller girls' books, and it appeared to her that the girls were like sisters, even though they weren't related.

This made an impact on Ella so much so that when she started her own school, she designed and implemented a uniform dress code with a Coat of Arms—a shield or crest that defined the school's values. Her design for Seed Daycare (which is still the Coat of Arms used at the daycare and its successor K-6 elementary school, Harvest Prep) is patterned after a Kenyan battle shield and has three images: the Baobab tree, the pyramids of Egypt, and the Okapi. Ella wanted to use artifacts that were symbolic of African and African-American people, their history, culture, and promise as a people.

The first image was the Baobab tree, reputed to be one of the largest, rarest, and oldest trees on earth, at times living thousands of years. Its bark, leaves, fruit, and trunk are all put to use. The bark is used by the indigenous people to make clothing and rope. The leaves are ground into a powder and used as both a condiment and medicine. The fruit, called monkey bread, is eaten. The flesh of the tree is used to make soap and dye. The trunk is used for water storage. Ella chose the Baobab tree because it is symbolic of the creativity of African-American people and their ability to adapt and to find ways to make the best out of what is available.

The second image was the three pyramids of Giza, Egypt. The largest of the three pyramids is the oldest of the seven wonders of the ancient world, dating to 2584 BCE, and the only ancient wonder still in existence. At 481 feet, the largest of the pyramids was the world's tallest man-made structure for over 3800 years. Ella chose the pyramids of Giza because they represent the mystery that continues to astound modern-day scientists and architects who are unable to figure out how the pyramids were built without any modern machinery and with such architectural precision. For Ella, the pyramids are symbolic of the same mystery that surrounds how African-American people were able to survive the Middle Passage when Africans were captured and traded as human cargo. The trans-Atlantic slave trade was the single largest movement of people in the history of mankind[6]. Between 10 million and 15 million Africans were forcibly transported across the Atlantic between 1500 and 1900; and, it is estimated that at least 2 million died during the Middle Passage. Those who survived were forced to undergo close to 400 years of brutal slavery. Yet, as Ella sees it, through all of this, African-Americans have survived and thrived – constantly evolving, holding firm to their foundation.

The third image for the shield was the Okapi—a zebra-like animal with a brown body and black-and-white striped legs. Although the Okapi's markings are reminiscent of the zebra, it is most closely related to the giraffe, although it has a much shorter neck. Ella chose the Okapi because African and African-American people span the color spectrum from black-and-white to all shades of brown.

When she returned home from Kenya, Ella had found a new mission and purpose. She would take the home daycare that she started in 1985 and start her own preschool. She told the small group of parents at her daycare of the revelations she received while on her trip.[7]

Soon this first group of parents began noticing a change in their children after being at Ella's daycare. They noticed a rise in their children's self-esteem, pride in their culture and heritage, and an increase in their cognitive growth. In 1987 Ella obtained a group family daycare license that allowed her to expand her home daycare to care for up to 14 children in her house. Word of mouth spread quickly about the success that the children were experiencing, and Ella began receiving daycare referrals from parents, neighbors, and community residents who heard of her reputation.

In 1987 Ella and Eric acquired a building to house the daycare center. However, it would take another three years to obtain the necessary permits, licenses, and financing to renovate the building as a daycare. Ella put this time to constructive use. She developed her own 40-week curriculum for preschool-age children that is still in use today. Finally, in 1990, Seed Academy preschool was born as a licensed daycare center and opened its first stand-alone building in north Minneapolis.

SEED, which stands for Success through Education and Evolutionary Development, was founded on the idea that children achieve success through a process that allows them to evolve as individuals. According to Ella, education, in particular for the poor and children of color, should be a well-planned and deliberate process. Seed's curriculum and educational process was a well-thought-out plan through which a child's development could evolve. Ella, a strong believer in her Christian faith, also believed that the name Seed was religiously symbolic. She said the Bible repeatedly talks about the importance of planting seeds, taking care in their planting, and nurturing their growth and development. These are the same principles that she applies in educating young children.

In 2005 the educational circle continued when Ella attended the University of St. Thomas in St. Paul, Minnesota, to study for her doctoral degree. Looking back on the road she has traveled, from the little girl from Aberdeen, Mississippi who was placed in special education because she stuttered, to the founder of schools that train and educate more than one thousand low-income children and children of color on a daily basis, Ella gives all of the praise to God. She now manages the Human Resources department for the various schools that she and her husband operate. Ella will begin law school in the fall of 2013.

### Eric Mahmoud

Known by one of his friends as the "Spartan," Eric maintains an unparalleled work schedule and regimen seven days a week. Each day he rises at 4:30 a.m., runs 6–7 miles, and follows the run with weight lifting. In 2013, at age 53, he completed his first 26.2-mile marathon, after having run a half marathon in 2012. While the school day at Harvest Prep and Best Academy ends at 5 p.m., he is typically at the school until late in the evening on weekdays and weekends, except when meetings and speaking engagements take him away. He is a hands-on administrator, actively involved with the student body, and can be regularly seen supervising students getting on and off the school buses at the beginning and end of each day. He lives on 4 or 5 hours of sleep each night, and friends and professional associates say they routinely receive e-mails sent between 2:00 a.m. and 4:00 a.m. In 2012 all of his hard work came to fruition when the State of Minnesota Department of Education named Harvest Prep and Best Academy as Reward Schools - two of the top-performing public schools in the State of Minnesota. In recognition of his outstanding work and contribution to the field of education, that same year Eric

Mahmoud was inducted into the National Charter School Hall of Fame at its annual convention in Minneapolis. In 2013 Best Academy, the boys-focused charter school he founded in 2008, received the National School Award from the Coalition of Schools Educating Boys of Color (COSEBOC) as one of the top five highest-performing schools for educating boys of color in the United States.

Eric grew up as Eric McLaughlin, Jr. in the hard-scrabble neighborhood of West Oak Lane, a lower-middle class, blue-collar neighborhood, bordering North Philadelphia. His father, Eric McLaughlin, Sr., was a maintenance worker for a plumbing company and a self-employed carpenter on the side. His mother, Annie McLaughlin, was an area sales manager for a Sears department store. Eric, Sr. and Annie instilled the spirit of self-determination and entrepreneurship in their children. Eric's younger brother lives in Atlanta, Georgia, and has his own landscaping and gardening business. Eric's oldest sister lives in South Bend, Indiana, where she owned a cleaning company and is working towards a Ph.D. in Divinity; and, Eric's younger sister operates her own hairstyling business and is also a real estate mogul in Philadelphia.

Eric started playing football at the age of 10 and in middle school became an avid weightlifter. At Dobbins High School in North Philadelphia he became a star football player and wrestler, but was often more concerned with making it home alive than with getting good grades. The North Philadelphia neighborhoods in which he attended middle school and high school in the late 70's were the scene of regular gang violence. The rate of rape, murder, and assault in Philadelphia increased dramatically in the 1970's, fueled by the drug epidemic and gang activity. North Philadelphia was the center of this activity.

As a teenager Eric noticed that none of the small businesses that flourished in his predominately working class African-American neighborhood were owned by African-Americans. They were White,

Arab, or Asian. He sensed that something was wrong. Here was a neighborhood in which 99% of the people living there were African-Americans, but none of them owned any of the businesses. He viewed it as a gross inequity that had to be remedied. He also distinctly remembers conversations with the teaching assistants at Wagner Middle School concerning these inequities and how conversations extended to such far-reaching topics as self-determination, community responsibility, and religion (he was agnostic at the time).

One day his father asked him, "Boy, what do you want to do with your life?" He thought a moment and recalled the dearth of African-American-owned businesses in his neighborhood and said, "I want to go into engineering and build a manufacturing plant in the neighborhood." Still in his teens Eric remembers walking down Ogontz Avenue, a busy street lined with small businesses, and being drawn into one of the many storefront religious establishments. There he heard an unusual message called "Do for Self," which spoke to African-Americans of self-determination and empowerment. This Do for Self message meant that African-Americans should get an education, start their own businesses, be responsible for their own well-being; and that African-American men, in particular, should be responsible for taking care of their women and children. It was a strange message that he had never heard before; or at least in this particular way. This principle would form one of the fundamental pillars of the responsibility that Eric felt as he pursued his college education, his engineering career after graduation, and then his transition into education, by addressing the educational dilemma facing low- income children.

At six-feet-three inches and close to 200 pounds, Eric was a standout football player and wrestler in high school. He was a starter on the varsity football team in his sophomore year, earning the distinction of being the defensive team's "monster back"—a defensive player who roams the field to find the point of attack—unlike every other defensive player who has an assigned area of responsibility. By his senior season, Eric was an All-City defensive end, garnering not just the respect and admiration of his young peers, but athletic scholarship offers from several colleges and universities, including Villanova and Swarthmore.

His football coaches were also the high school wrestling coaches, and they talked him into trying out for wrestling, too. Head Coach Smith (Coach Smitty) was a father-like figure to Eric and his teammates, regularly taking them outside the city to suburban and other places to watch college football games on Saturdays, which Eric found particularly enjoyable.

As a star athlete Eric was somewhat protected from the gang violence that proliferated in Philadelphia; gang members took a hands-off approach towards athletes. However, the protection from gang violence did not extend to other dangers that existed in Philadelphia. Eric was 17 years old when he was riding on a city subway train with two of his high school teammates on their way downtown to a Temple University football game. While his two friends were joking and laughing at a man on the train, who was obviously intoxicated, Eric suddenly found a rusty straight-edge razor at his throat. Reacting instinctively, he dispatched the intoxicated man, but found himself trembling and shaken the rest of the day. Eric knew then that he wanted to get as far away from Philadelphia and Pennsylvania as he could.

While many local colleges and universities offered him athletic scholarships, with the prospect of a career in sports, Eric wanted to challenge the stereotype that the only way a young Black man could get to college was through sports. Another university acknowledged his academic skills—after all, he graduated second in his class—the University of Wisconsin, Madison. He accepted a full academic scholarship to pursue a degree in engineering with the chance to work summers at Boeing Aircraft in Seattle, Proctor & Gamble in Green Bay, Wisconsin, and Honeywell Corporation in Minneapolis.

Soon after Eric began work on an engineering degree (nurturing his dream of starting his own manufacturing plant in the African-American community), he also immersed himself in African-American history and culture. He wanted to learn the history of his people and what caused their current condition.

In the 1970's and 1980's, the University of Wisconsin, Madison, was a very liberal, liberal arts college. The environment encouraged expansion of ideas. Campus demonstrations were the order of the day during the Civil Rights and Vietnam War movements of the 1960s and 70s. During Eric's matriculation from 1979 to 1983, the university environment was a cauldron of ideologies, philosophies, and alternatives to the norm. Various schools of thought, from Socialism, to Communism to White Supremacy, and Black Nationalism were heard on campus. In fact, Eric and Ella met during their work on campus with the International Committee against Racism (INCAR). It was an experience that would help shape his thinking.

In addition to frequently attending meetings of INCAR, Eric was on the Black Student Association (BSA) committee. One of its purposes was to bring to campus renowned African-American speakers, such as Dr. Naim Akbar, Haki Madhubuti, and Dr. Amos Wilson. Dr. Akbar, a psychologist and professor at Florida State University, talked about the psychological impact of slavery on the African-American psyche and the importance that culture played in the rehabilitation from that devastation.

At one point in the talk, Dr. Akbar told his predominantly African-American student audience to look at the images all around them in Rathskeller Hall (the UW student union). He said those images of German culture and heritage reaffirmed the history and culture of the German people as an institutional structure. Dr. Akbar challenged the African-American students in attendance to create institutions that affirmed their own culture and heritage. Dr. Akbar did not imply that

Blacks or African-Americans should separate themselves from mainstream culture; but rather, they should establish parity between their culture and the culture of those around them. This would reaffirm the importance of inclusion as part of the fabric of the larger American culture.

Another lecture Eric attended was given by prominent African-American journalist and activist, Lou Palmer, who wrote for the *Chicago American, Chicago Daily News* and *Chicago Defender*. Its central idea was that the primary role of education was to instill the principles and values of the educational institution and culture of which the students were a part. Mr. Palmer took learning reading, writing, and arithmetic as the tools necessary to perpetuate the institution and its culture.

Eric recalls Haki Madhubuti, poet, publisher, and owner of Third World Press and Book Store, who had published extensively on African-American culture. During his presentation Madhubuti emphasized the importance of self-education, self-reliance, and educating African-American children in the importance of culture and community; more specifically, focusing on the need for independent thinking created by a culture that allowed children to see themselves in the education they were receiving. One of his short treatises, "African-Centered Education, its Value, Importance and Necessity in the Development of Black Children,"[8] provided an historical account of Black people in America and the struggle they had waged for education. Madhubuti spoke of the importance of culture and the specific things that could be done to instill in children the importance of education, community, service, and promoting social relationships between African-Americans and other people.

Dr. Amos N. Wilson, Assistant Professor of Psychology at New York University and author of numerous works, wrote the seminal study "Developmental Psychology of the Black Child."[9] Its thesis was that the psyche of African-American children had been negatively shaped by their American experience. He cited numerous studies that identified the developmental superiority, rather than inferiority, of African-American children and how the impact of their American educational experience had slowed the innate development of Black children. He gave examples of African-centered preschools that prepared children to read and compute at the level of first-, second- and third-graders. According to Wilson, when White five-year-old children were asked about their identities, they rarely talked about their skin color, but about their family history, their culture, and religion. But when five-year-old Black children were asked about their identities, they referred to their skin color in negative terms. Dr. Wilson posited that African-Americans needed to establish institutions of learning that would restore the natural intelligence of African-American children and reestablish their positive self-identity.

Eric's involvement with the Black Student Association and hearing these African-American thought leaders helped give shape to his teenage idea of starting his own business. After graduation he thought, 'Now that I have all of this historical knowledge and theory, what am I going to do with it?'

In 1983, after graduating from the University of Wisconsin, Eric moved to Minneapolis and joined Ella, who was working at a daycare center in south Minneapolis. Ella soon became the director of the daycare center and Eric, who began his career in engineering at the Fortune 500 companies Medtronic and Honeywell, became a member of the daycare center's board of directors.

In the meantime Eric continued studying African-American history and culture, now under the tutelage of Mahmoud El-Kati, Professor Emeritus of African-American History at Macalester College in St. Paul, Minnesota. El-Kati remains a frequent lecturer, writer, and commentator on the African-American experience.

The African-American history Eric learned while studying with Professor El-Kati transformed his life. For example, he learned that 30-35% of Africans brought to America during the slave trade were Muslims. Islam began to provide answers to questions he had long pondered. In 1984 Eric McLaughlin converted to Islam and became Eric Mahmoud. The influence of Muslims in his hometown of Philadelphia finally culminated in Eric's new personal and spiritual commitment. He became part of Philadelphia's long history, starting in the early 1900s, of African-Americans converting to the religion of Islam. According to several estimates, Philadelphia has surpassed Detroit and New York City and is now home to the largest population of African-American Muslims in the United States.[10]

Eric pursued his career in engineering, with the goal of establishing his own community economic development business. But it became increasingly clear to him that education was the foundation and driving force behind community economic development: If you give someone a fish, as the Chinese proverb goes, they can eat for a day; but if you teach them how to fish, they can eat for lifetime. Eric had found his mission.

*Education is the medium by which a people are prepared for the creation of their own particular civilization.*

—*Marcus Garvey*

### Evolutionaries

After the success the Mahmouds experienced with Seed Daycare in the mid-to late 1980s, the logical progression was to establish an elementary school, to harvest the seeds they had planted in the daycare. In 1992 Harvest Preparatory School was established as a private school for children in grades K through 6th. Harvest Prep, as it is known today, was originally started as a private, nonprofit elementary school under the umbrella of Seed Daycare, Inc. and opened its doors to 24 students. Seven years later it became a separate

501(c)(3) nonprofit corporation. Enrollment in Harvest Prep grew from 24 students in 1992 to more than 400 students today with an annual waiting list. From their inception, Seed Daycare and Harvest Prep focused on teaching fundamental skills in reading, math, and science, and on engaging parents in their children's learning, helping them to develop cultural knowledge, pride, and self-confidence.

*We are the best, not because we say it, but because the best is what we do.*

— *Best Academy School Creed*

Sixteen years after Harvest Prep, Best Academy was established, a gender-separate charter school for boys and girls, grades K-8. BEST (which originally stood for "Boys in Engineering, Science, and Technology"), was started to address the unique educational needs of boys.

Several educational researchers, including Michael Gurian (*Minds of Boys*)[11] and Jawanza Kunjufu, (*Keeping Black Boys Out of Special Education*)[12] had demonstrated that boys and girls have different learning styles.

In December 2005 Eric Mahmoud was in a book store and started reading Dr. Kunjufu's book, *Keeping Black Boys Out of Special Education*. He was quickly mesmerized. Dr. Kunjufu's research showed that boys were slower than girls in developing reading skills, and for African-American boys, this often resulted in them being classified as slow and being placed in special education classes. According to Kunjufu 80% of students recommended for special education are below grade level in reading. In the case of boys, this didn't necessarily indicate a cognitive deficit, but rather an aversion of boys towards reading, and the need to focus on reading as an essential tool for learning. In general, wrote Kunjufu, boys are more aggressive, have higher energy levels, shorter attention spans, and slower maturation rates. They are generally less cooperative. As teens they grow larger than girls, their gross motor skills are more developed than their fine motor skills, and their hearing is inferior to that of girls. Boys have a greater interest in math than reading. They're not as neat as girls, they're louder, have bigger, more sensitive egos, and they are more influenced by their peer group.

Halfway through the book, Eric had made up his mind that he was going to start a boys' academy to address their unique learning styles. Boys in north Minneapolis, where Harvest Prep and Best Academy are located, face the most significant academic challenges of students anywhere in Minnesota or the United States.

The same year the Best boys program was created, 2008, parents asked that a gender-separate program for girls be developed as well. The very next year, Sister Academy—Sisters in Science, Technology, Engineering and Rx (medicine)—was started as an all-girls program, grades 5 through 8, under the Best Academy school charter.

*Teach a boy, you teach an individual; teach a girl, and you teach a whole nation.*

*—Mahatma Gandhi*

While one of the immediate educational crises in north Minneapolis, and indeed nationally, is the plight of African-American boys, Eric and Ella Mahmoud recognized that the long-term vitality of all communities and societies depends on the education of girls. In most instances mothers are the primary caregivers and educators of young children; they are the ones who have the greatest impact on the educational outcomes of children. Following Gandhi's belief, international programs such as Room to Read[13] —which opened schools in countries with extremely low literacy rates—focus on the education of girls.

In low-income communities, the importance of mothers is especially keen. In north Minneapolis, where Harvest Prep and Best Academy are located, more than half of the families are headed by females, and 20-25% of the families are either homeless or highly mobile. Digging deeper, most of the female heads of households for elementary school-age children are under 30 years of age. It is likely that these young mothers have no education past high school. While it can honestly be said that the overwhelming majority of these mothers want what is best for their children, many lack basic background knowledge to provide their children with a solid academic start. These parents may also lack the skill to keep their children academically competitive for the 21st century classroom environment, where there are more demands on students and parents than ever before.

Thus, understanding and educating the young mothers of children from low-income backgrounds is also vital to the success of any school. Educational leaders must help mothers understand the critical importance of education in their children's lives (see Chapter 2). They must understand the severe social costs associated with the lack of an adequate education. School leaders and educators must be cognizant of all the factors that affect the lives of low-income children and must intentionally plan to address them. Thus, having personnel assigned to parent and family engagement is critical. A child psychologist, either on staff or as a consultant, is required. Frequent school assemblies— to engage parents and families and make them aware of the school culture and the importance of academic achievement in the lives of their children—are required. Finally, having personnel who are culturally aware, who have insight into the multiple struggles faced by these young mothers, other family members, and the children—is essential.

## Establishment of Best East

In the fall of 2009, members of the East African Somali community in Minneapolis approached Eric and Ella Mahmoud to ask if they would consider starting a school to meet the unique cultural and academic needs of their burgeoning English language learner (ELL) community. The No Child Left Behind (NCLB) law passed by Congress in 2001, and Title I of the Elementary and Secondary Education Act, specifically recognizes the barriers faced by ELL students in closing the educational achievement gap, and authorized the development and creation of programs that address the specific needs of such students.

Colonial rule had divided the Somali people from the mid-1800s until 1960, when two territories were reunited to form what is now known as Somalia. The relatively new post-colonial Somali government fell in 1991 after opposition from clan-based militias and three years of civil war. During the ensuing civil war, there had been no effective government in Somalia, and over one million of its people have fled to refugee camps in neighboring Ethiopia, Kenya, Djibouti, Yemen, and Burundi. Resettlement programs have enabled refugee families to move to Germany, Switzerland, Finland, and England in Europe, and to states like Minnesota in the United States. Minnesota, known for its resettlement of Hmong refugees in the 1980s, now has the highest population of Somalis anywhere outside of Somalia itself.

For many students of these Minnesota families, English is a second language (ESL). Although American culture has become engrained in our educational system, from the pledge of allegiance to the "Star-Spangled Banner," other cultures are rarely recognized or treated as factors in our educational system. Where a student's community and family culture is substantially different from the dominant culture, culture becomes a very important component of student learning. It represents who we are as a people, as well as our goals and aspirations. It includes language, food, dress, customs, and habits.

We have seen the disparate educational effects of this lack of recognition in Native American, Hispanic, and African-American populations. It is no coincidence that each of these groups ranked at or near the bottom of the educational— and thus the socioeconomic—ladder.

Some aspects of the Somali culture are unique and foreign to the traditional American culture. One example is the way that Somali and some other East African women dress: long dresses and skirts and a head covering. Interestingly, if we were able to go back 50-100 years in American history, we would find similar dress for women – particularly those who had recently migrated to the United States. Eastern European women, in particular, often wore long dresses and a head covering called a babushka. Yet there is an aversion to this type of dress in American culture today.

Another example is the foods Somalis eat. Most don't eat pork so if pepperoni pizza is being served for lunch in the public school system, there is a problem. More culturally familiar foods have to be offered. No longer can everyone be expected to eat the same American food, which often has hidden and unintended consequences.

Finally, the cultural values, traditions, and practices of Somali families vary greatly from those in America. By American standards Somali women are often considered to be in subservient roles, yet Somali women are the ones in control of their children's education. Unlike American culture, after children reach puberty, there is very little public mixing between the sexes. To the extent that the children go to school and adopt American customs and habits, this is a two-way street. On the one hand, it may indicate their assimilation; on the other hand, it may create conflict at home where parents and families are either unfamiliar with, or do not accept, American culture.

In 2010 Best Academy East was opened to create an environment that respects these cultural differences to help to make students and parents more comfortable with the educational experience. The more comfortable the parents are with the educational experience, the more invested they become in their children's education and the more effective teachers can be in educating the children. By 2012 this recognition began to reap dividends in the children's academic achievement.

The most recent addition to the Seed-Harvest lineage is the new Mastery School. In February 2012, under the leadership of Minneapolis Public Schools Superintendent Bernadeia Johnson, the Minneapolis School Board authorized the creation of four Mastery Schools. The Mastery Schools will operate under the leadership of Eric Mahmoud and his administrative team. The purpose of this unique district/charter collaboration is to offer as many high-performing school options as possible for children with the greatest educational needs in Minneapolis. The first Mastery School opened its doors in August of 2012 for 150 children in grades K-2, and will add a grade each year until it reaches K-8. Once the first Mastery School has proven successful, the additional Mastery Schools will come online.

**Where We are Today**

Beginning with ten preschool students in 1985, the Seed-Harvest lineage now has a total enrollment of more than 1,200 students in five separate academic programs: Harvest Prep, Best Academy, Sister Academy, Best East, and the new Mastery School. The mission of all of these schools is to instruct, empower, enable, and guide children to achieve superior academic, social, and moral development.

In 2012 Best Academy was considered the highest rated school in the state of Minnesota according to the state's newly implemented Multiple Measurement Rating (MMR) system for schools with over 80% free and reduced lunch populations; Harvest Prep was just slightly lower. The MMR measures proficiency, student growth, achievement gap reduction, and graduation rates. Schools earn points in each category. Both Best Academy and Harvest Prep were designated by the State of Minnesota as "Reward Schools," an award given to the highest performing 15% of Title I schools in the state. Figure 2 represents where public schools in Minneapolis rank.

In the far upper-right corner is Best Academy, representing the school with the highest proficiency and highest growth in Minneapolis. Close behind is Harvest Prep. However, directly across the street from Harvest Prep and Best Academy and in the neighborhood surrounding Best Academy and Harvest Prep are some of the lowest performing schools in the entire state. Virtually all of the schools in north Minneapolis are located in the lower-left portion of the plot map, which means that they have the lowest proficiency and lowest student growth in the city, yet these schools draw from the same student population and the same families as Best Academy and Harvest Prep. The words of Eric Mahmoud echo, *The challenge of educating Black children is not a hardware problem, but rather a software problem. There's nothing wrong with the hardware (i.e. the intellectual capacity of the children); the problem is the wrong software is being used to program them for success.*

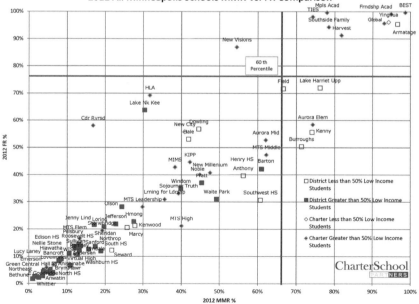

Figure 2. 2012 All Minneapolis Schools MMR vs. Free-and-Reduced Lunch Comparison (Courtesy of Charter School Partners)

# 2

# The Social Costs of the Achievement Gap

*It is easier to build strong children than to repair broken men.*
*—Frederick Douglass*

## Case Study 2: Hakim

Hakim had been in and out of foster care in Louisville, Kentucky, before arriving at Best Academy in 2009. His mother had been involved in prostitution. Hakim remembers strange men walking past him while he was watching television in the living room, heading to his mother's bedroom. On several different occasions between 2003 and 2009, child protection authorities removed Hakim from the home. His attendance at school was sporadic, and his academic progress suffered.

Hakim's mother died in 2009 when he was 10 years old, and he was sent to live with his aunt and uncle in Minneapolis, who enrolled him in Best Academy as a 5th grader. He was at least two grade levels behind in math and three grade levels behind in reading according to pre-assessment testing. Despite life circumstances, Hakim was a mature and respectful young man with a thirst for knowledge. His aunt and uncle recognized this spark of desire and intelligence within and wanted to enroll him in the best school possible.

After completing a nine-hour school day at Best Academy, Hakim spent hours on homework, a new and a not-so-pleasant experience with which he struggled mightily. He had to spend 1-1/2 to 2 hours reading each day. There was no television or playing video games during the week. On the morning commute to school, Hakim would pull out his math book, and he and his uncle would solve math problems. On Saturdays Hakim got four hours of math tutoring. Hakim's aunt and uncle used every available opportunity for learning. They took him on trips; they took him to community events involving art, music, and public speaking; they helped him see the importance of understanding his own rich culture and history.

After just 12 weeks at Best Academy, Hakim began to show signs of progress in both reading and math. By the time he was three-fourths of the way through his first school year, Hakim was predicting proficiency in both reading and math. In the space of seven months, he had progressed two full grade levels in math and three full grade levels in reading. In May 2010, less than 10 months after enrolling at Best Academy, Hakim's Minnesota Comprehensive Assessment test results showed that, in fact, he had exceeded state standards in reading and met state standards in math. By the 6th grade at Best Academy, Hakim was a member of the school's Junior National Honor Society, the school basketball and wrestling teams, and the student council.

There are hundreds and thousands of Hakims waiting for our educational system to recognize their intrinsic intelligence, their spark of human potential, and to do what is necessary to educate them. It is our responsibility as adults in this society to find the resources, including talented educators and school leaders, to educate these children.

### The Social Costs of the Achievement Gap

Never in our nation's history have the demands on our educational system been greater nor the consequences of failure so severe. Beyond the high-stakes accountability requirements mandated by state and federal laws, the difference between success and failure in school is, literally, life and death for many students.[14]

More than most states, Minnesota has an education-dependent economy. According to the Georgetown Center on Education and the Workforce, by 2018, 70% of the jobs in Minnesota will require some form of postsecondary training.[15] By contrast, only 40% of today's workforce needs a postsecondary credential.[16] In Minneapolis and St. Paul public schools, 70-75% of the students are ethnic minorities. Given the changing ethnic face of our school-aged population, most of the students who make up this employment gap are African-American, Latino, and Native American.

Despite record-high levels of unemployment in Minnesota and nationally in 2012, employers whose jobs require a postsecondary education cannot find enough qualified workers locally to fill them. Employers with jobs that require a higher degree of education and training no longer find Minnesota the fertile employment environment it once was. It is no coincidence that many of the highly-skilled engineering jobs and jobs that require advanced degrees are being filled by immigrants from India, Asia, and the Middle East. We are truly living and operating in a global economy.

Today, a child who graduates from high school with a mastery of essential knowledge and skills is prepared to compete in the global marketplace with numerous pathways of opportunity. For students who fail in our educational system, there are virtually no pathways of opportunity. Their likely path includes poverty, incarceration, poor health, and/or dependence on society's welfare systems. Poverty, incarceration, mental, and physical health are all inextricably intertwined with a person's level of education.

According to data from the Minnesota State Office of Demography, less than 50% of all African-American children graduated from high school in 2010, the lowest graduation rate for African-American children in the entire country. Conversely, White students in Minnesota have one of the highest graduation rates in the United States at 85%. Here is an overview of the sobering statistics associated with an inadequate education.

### Poverty

According to Servaas van der Berg,[17] author of *Poverty and Education,*[18] educational and economic research have yielded two consistent findings on the relationship between education and poverty: (a) home background or socioeconomic status (meaning education, occupation, and income) is an important determinant of educational outcomes, and (b) education strongly affects earnings.

Poverty is not simply the absence of financial resources; it is the lack of capability to function effectively in society.[19] Therefore, inadequate education can be considered a form of poverty. Absolute poverty, which means the absence of adequate resources, hampers learning through deficits in parental education, nutrition, health, and home circumstances (a lack of books, bad lighting, or a place to do homework). Absolute poverty discourages enrollment in school, reduces learning in school and leaves survival to the higher grades in jeopardy. *Relative poverty,* on the other hand, means exclusion from the mainstream in rich countries, a state that can reduce the motivation of the relatively poor and their ability to gain the full benefits of education.[20]

Education can reduce poverty in a number of ways. First, the better educated people are, the more likely they are to get jobs, be more productive, and earn more. Education, particularly of girls, brings social benefits that improve the conditions of the poor, for example, it lowers the fertility rate, improves the health care of children, and affords women greater participation in the labor market. Students' home background is the single most important factor influencing educational outcomes. Poverty is strongly correlated with a range of other home background variables, including income, wealth, homelessness, family stability, home ownership, and parental educational attainment.[21]

In the United States, at the turn of the 21st century, 44 million Americans could not read a newspaper or fill out a job application.[22] Another 50 million could not read or comprehend above the eighth grade level.[23] Close to half (43%) of people with the lowest literacy skills live below the government's official poverty line.[24] Research shows that poverty, and hence the lack of education, are associated with a higher risk of a multitude of negative outcomes for children, including low income, incarceration, and poor physical and mental health.

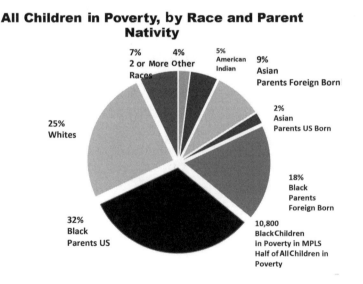

Figure 3. All children in Minneapolis in Poverty, by Race and Parent Nativity

According to the 2011 *One Minneapolis* report commissioned by The Minneapolis Foundation, in Minnesota's largest city, Minneapolis, 1 out of every 3 children – close to 22,400 - lives in poverty. More than half of all the Native American, Asian, and African-American children live in poverty. Fifty percent of the children living in poverty are Black – 32% African-American and 18% foreign born. The 10,800 Black children living in poverty in Minneapolis vastly outnumber the children of all other races – almost equaling all other races combined.[25] In sheer numbers, there are more Black families in Minneapolis living in poverty than any other racial or ethnic group, including Whites.

### School Dropouts

According to the U. S. government report, *The State of Literacy in America; Estimates at the Local, State and National Levels*, (1998), over 90 million adults in the United States, nearly one out of two, were functionally illiterate or near illiterate, and without the minimum skills required in a modern society.[26] An astounding 82% of prison inmates were school dropouts!

## Dropouts Among Prison Inmates in America

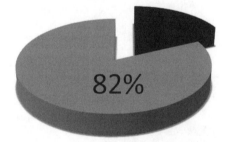

Figure 4. Dropouts Among Prison Inmates in America, 1998

Reading proficiency by the end of third grade is often a predictor of future academic and life success. Through the third grade most students are learning to read, whereas, in the fourth grade they begin reading to learn, to gain information, and think critically. The ability to read and comprehend what is read becomes a gateway to understanding in all other subject areas. About three-fourths of students who are poor readers in third grade will remain poor readers by the time they get to high school.[27] Students with limited reading skills are more likely to exhibit behavioral problems, to repeat a grade, and eventually to drop out. In Minneapolis based on 2011 MCA data, African-American students were tied with American Indian students for the 2nd from the bottom lowest third-grade reading proficiency of all other ethnic group – almost 100% lower than White students.

## MPS 3rd Grade Proficiency in Reading by Ethnicity (English Proficient Students)

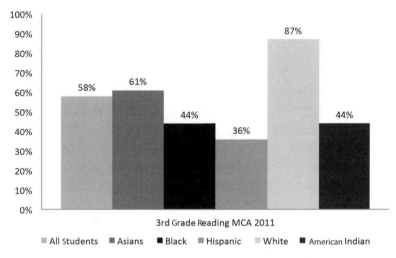

Figure 5. MPS 3rd Grade Proficiency in Reading by Ethnicity (English Proficient Students), 2011.

### Lifetime Earnings by Educational Attainment

According to a 2009 study conducted by Georgetown University,[28] median lifetime earnings rise steadily for workers with increasing educational attainment. Overall, the median lifetime earnings for all workers are $1.7 million, or just under $42,000 per year ($20 per hour). Over a 40-year career, those who didn't earn a high school diploma or GED are expected to bring in less than $1 million, which translates into slightly more than $24,000 a year ($11.70 per hour). Obtaining a high school diploma adds 33% more to lifetime earnings compared to that of a dropout; the average annual earnings of those with a high school diploma is $32,600 ($15.67 per hour). Clearly, the economic penalty for not finishing high school is steep — almost $9,000 a year.

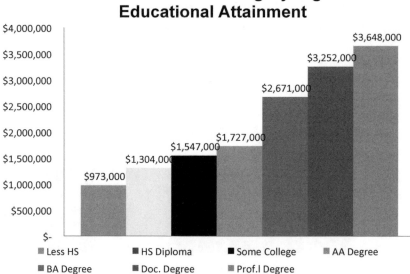

Figure 6. Median Lifetime Earnings by Highest Educational Attainment, 2009.

On average, students with a bachelor's degree earn $1.7 million more over their lifetime than students who drop out of school and almost $1.4 million more than students with a high school degree. The greater the educational disparity, the larger the earnings disparity, with a whopping $2.675 million gap between the average earnings of a student with a professional degree and a student who drops out of school.

### Incarceration

The United States holds the distinction of being the world leader in incarcerating its citizens; with the exception of Russia and South Africa, its imprisonment rates are 6 to 10 times that of most industrialized nations.[29] According to the 2007 report issued by the U.S. Department of Education entitled *Literacy Behind Bars: Results From the 2003 National Assessment of Adult Literacy Prison Survey*, on average, over 60% of prison inmates were in the lowest two categories of literacy assessment (below basic and basic); 36.3% were intermediate category; and, only 3.3% were considered proficient. Furthermore, on average, over 85% of prison inmates who dropped out of school before completing high school were in the lowest two categories of literacy assessment (below basic and basic);15% were intermediate; and none were proficient.[30]

### Prison Inmates Reading Below the 4th Grade Level

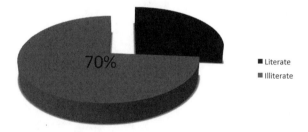

Figure 7. Prison Inmates Reading Below the 4th Grade Level, 1998.

According to the U. S. government report, *The State of Literacy in America; Estimates at the Local, State and National Levels*, (1998), the average reading level of children in juvenile correction institutions was that of a 4th grader.[31] While the incidence of learning disabilities among the general population was roughly 5%, it was estimated that 50% of those in the criminal justice system have learning disabilities.[32]

A 2005 study conducted by University of California–Berkeley economist, Enrico Moretti,[33] found that a 10% increase in the high school graduation rate would likely reduce the murder and assault arrest rates in this country by approximately 20%.[34] The same study found that increasing the high school completion rate by just 1% for men, ages 20-60, would save the United States up to $1.4 billion per year in reduced costs from crime.

In 2010 it cost $7,161 a year to educate a child in Minnesota,[35] but about $75,000 to incarcerate a juvenile and $50,000 to incarcerate an adult. In other words, it costs 10 times more to care for an incarcerated juvenile as it does to educate that juvenile, and 7 times more to care for an incarcerated adult.[36]

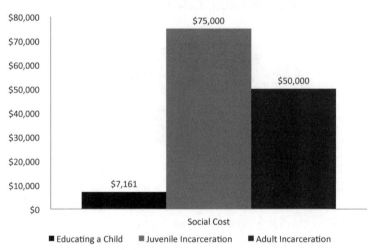

### Education is s Sound Investment
### Cost of Education vs Incarceration

Figure 8. Education is a Sound Investment/Cost of Education vs. Incarceration, 2010.

**Welfare**

There is also a strong correlation between education and welfare participation. Those with the lowest levels of educational attainment are more likely to receive welfare benefits, and 75% of those claiming welfare are functionally illiterate.[37] In Oregon, which has studied the fiscal return on education, almost two-thirds of welfare recipients have no more than a high school diploma.[38]

## Literacy of Among Welfare Recipients in U.S.

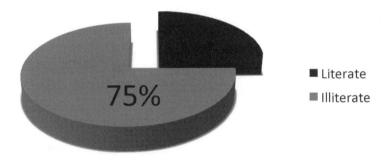

Figure 9. Literacy of Among Welfare Recipients in U.S., 1993

**Employment and Wealth**

The "employment gap" is the difference in the percentage of working-age adults, by race, who are working. Among U.S. metropolitan areas, the Twin Cities has one of the highest rates of adults working. However, in 2011 it had the single largest gap in employment between Whites and Blacks and Native Americans, compared to any other major metropolitan area in the country according to the Economic Policy Institute, a non-partisan Washington, D.C. think tank.

Census Bureau figures show that in 2010 the median household net worth (as distinguished from income) for White Americans was $110,729; for African Americans it was $4,995 – a difference of 2,200%. Studies show that the wealth gap between Whites and African-Americans has more than quadrupled over the course of the last generation.[39,149]

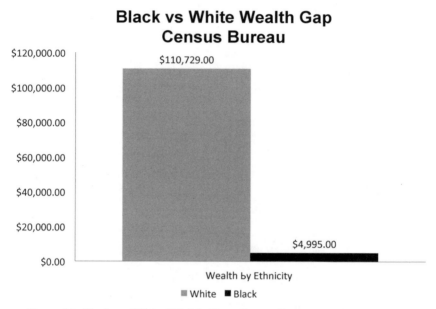

Figure 10. Black vs. White Wealth Gap, Census Bureau 2010.

### The Achievement Gap and the Economy

Consider this hypothetical statement from the 2009 *McKinsey* report on education: "If the United States had in recent years closed the gap between its educational achievement levels and those of better performing nations such as Finland and Korea, Gross Domestic Production (GDP) in 2008 could have been $1.3 trillion to $2.3 trillion higher. This represents 9 to 16% of GDP." According to noted educational authority, Dr. Steve Perry,[40] it means that if the country as a whole performed better academically, we would have brought in enough money to erase much of the nation's deficit. In some respects, then, the American education crisis is an American economic crisis.

According to the Bureau of Labor Statistics, in May 2012, the nation's unemployment rate was 8.2%. However, the jobless rate for Whites was below the national average, at 7.4%, while the rate for African Americans was nearly twice that, at 13.6%. Disaggregated by gender, the picture for Black males was even bleaker, at 15%.

Teenagers between the ages of 16 and 19 experienced the highest levels of joblessness of all, particularly youth of color: for White teens the rate was 23.5%, but for Latino youths it was 31% and for Black teens, 44.2%.

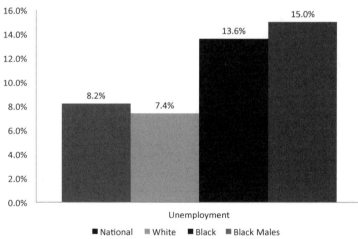

Figure 11. National Unemployment Rates, 2012.

As Frederick Douglass stated more than 100 years ago, "It is easier to build strong children than to repair broken men." The social costs of failing to educate children are enormous. Children who do not receive an adequate education are much more likely to drop out of school and end up in our criminal justice system, where, as stated previously, it costs 10 times more annually to incarcerate a juvenile, than it does to educate a juvenile, and 7 times more to incarcerate an adult. Even if the child manages to avoid our criminal justice system, they are much more likely to show up in other sectors that pose a drain on our economy and society, such as welfare. It is projected that by 2018, 70% of the jobs in our economy will require a post-secondary education. Given the fact that 70-75% of the children in Minneapolis and St. Paul public schools are ethnic minorities that means that these are the students that must fill those jobs. It is, therefore, incumbent upon us to educate them.

# 3

## The Prototype for Success - Harvest Prep

*History is a clock that tells people their political and cultural time of day.*

*- John Henrik Clarke*

### Case Study 3: Aquila

Aquila, a 7th grader, transferred to Sister Academy from a prestigious private school in the Minneapolis area. Both of her parents were African-American professionals with advanced degrees, but they were distressed about her seeming lack of interest in school. Her mother described her as a "contrarian." If you said "up" she would say "down". If you said "go right" she would go left. Eric Mahmoud met with Aquila and her parents one night at their home. Aquila was wearing white-framed sunglasses – at night, inside the house. The parents decided they wanted their daughter at Sister Academy. Eric was glad Aquila would be coming to his school, but he knew it would be a challenge - thinking to himself, 'This is going to be a tough nut to crack.'

When the year began, it was clear that Aquila had a difficult time with authority. Mr. Mahmoud wondered if she could accept the rules, regimen, and discipline of Sister Academy and if Aquila might report her parents to Child Protective Services for subjecting her to such a rigid and restrictive school system.

A few months went by—stormy months—but then the clouds broke, and the sun began to shine. Aquila discovered a cultural affinity with the other young women at Sister Academy that she had not experienced before; the same sisterhood that Ella Mahmoud observed 25 years earlier among the school-aged girls in Nairobi, Kenya. Among young women who looked like her and who had the same cultural background, Aquila came to enjoy the academic rigor and the competition for excellence. One day Aquila came home and told her parents that Sister Academy was "the best school for her". Their jaws dropped. After figuratively picking themselves up off of the floor, Aquila's parents could see that Aquila's motivation and attitude towards school had changed dramatically. Aquila, the 7th grader, told her parents that she wanted the 8th grade math books for Christmas so she could get a head start on next year! The contrarian would become an amazing scholar, and her state standardized test scores at Sister exceeded her performance at the private school.

### Background Data on Minneapolis School-Age Children

According to the 2011 *One Minneapolis* report published by The Minneapolis Foundation, African-American and Native American children are at the highest risk of academic failure based on attendance, suspensions, kindergarten readiness, reading at the third-grade level, and student engagement.[41] Attendance, suspensions, and kindergarten readiness will be discussed below. Third grade reading and student engagement are discussed more fully throughout the book.

## Minneapolis Public Schools Attendance by Ethnicity

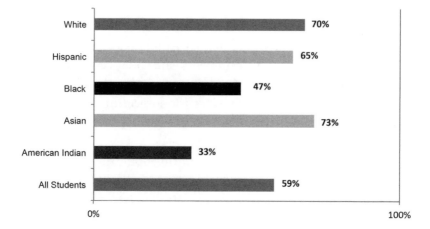

Figure 12. Minneapolis Public Schools Attendance by Ethnicity, 2010.

## Attendance

African-American and Native American children have the lowest attendance rates in the city. And if children are not in school, they're not learning.

## Suspensions

African-American and Native American students have the highest rates of suspension from school in Minneapolis. In fact, African-American students are being suspended at a rate six times greater and Native American students are suspended at a rate four times greater than that of White students. Moreover, African-American students who are suspended are more likely to have more than one suspension from school each year. Efforts are underway in Minneapolis Public Schools to correct this severe imbalance, including behavioral awareness and cultural competency training. Both involve understanding the family backgrounds of the children and the culture that forms their frame of reference. Many of our children are exposed to conditions that tend to be uncommon in the larger culture, including absentee fathers, incarcerated fathers and male relatives,

**Students with One or More Suspensions During School Year by Ethnicity**

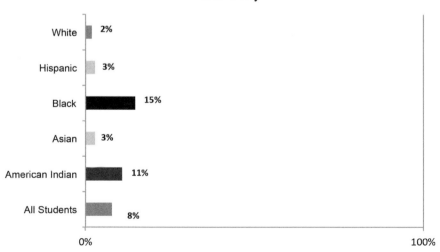

Figure 13. Students with One or More Suspensions During School Year by Ethnicity, 2009-2010.

domestic abuse, substance abuse, gang-related activity, homelessness, and so on.

Many of these conditions have become the accepted norm in the subculture from which many of these children come. They prompt behaviors that are natural responses to these traumatic conditions, such as fighting, defiance to authority, tardiness, and absenteeism. As one expert in family counseling put it, "Because of the traumatic conditions to which these children are exposed, if they didn't act out, there would be something wrong with them." This is one side of the equation.

The other side is that often the primary institutional response to their behavior is punitive. When students manifest behaviors that are considered inappropriate for the school environment, rather than trying to understand the conditions that gave rise to these behaviors, the institutional response is to punish. This suspension imbalance is due, in part, to the failure to recognize the underlying conditions which are causing the student behavior, and an unconscious bias on the part of teachers and administrators in public schools, which penalizes low-income students of color more severely for the same behavior as engaged in by their White and more affluent counterparts.

In Minneapolis this unconscious bias produces suspension rates for African-American students that are six times greater than White students, and twice the national average. By now the reader may see that Minneapolis shows a trend in Black/White racial disparities as a result of this unconscious bias. It has a Black/White suspension rate that is twice the national average; it has one of the highest Black/White academic gaps in the country; and it has the highest Black/White employment gap in the country.

To be sure, there are cultural and demographic behavioral differences between student populations and the teachers that serve them. In the Minneapolis Public Schools the teachers are overwhelmingly White, middle class, and female; whereas the population of Minneapolis Public Schools is predominantly low-income students of color, with the single largest group being African-American and African immigrant students. This demographic and cultural disconnect between teachers and students have led to the disproportionate discipline of African-American students.

The same disciplinary issues exist at Harvest Prep and Best Academy. Harvest Prep and Best Academy provide training for staff to try to prepare them for the unique challenges in working in an urban environment. Additional mental health and family support services are employed to reduce the number of suspensions of students. More prevention strategies will be discussed in depth in Chapter 6, but the objective is not to put children out of school but to keep them in school. Putting them out of school, in too many cases, only returns them to the environment that caused the disruptive behavior in the first place.

### Kindergarten Readiness

Children who start school behind are more likely to stay behind and fall further behind as they move up the grades. According to the The Minneapolis Foundation's 2011 *One Minneapolis* report, there was close to a 100% difference between the reading scores of 3rd grade White and Black students in Minneapolis. By 10th grade the Black/White reading gap was even greater. Each of these benchmarks is a predictor of lifelong outcomes.

In Minneapolis Hispanic, Native American, and African-American children have the lowest rates of kindergarten school readiness compared to Whites students.

Only slightly more than 40% of Hispanic students, less than two-thirds of Native American students, and slightly more than two-thirds of African-American students are ready for kindergarten, compared

**Kindergarten Readiness by Ethnicity, Minneapolis Public Schools**

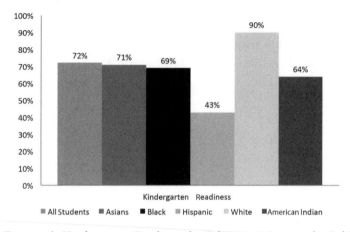

Figure 14. Kindergarten Readiness by Ethnicity, Minneapolis Public Schools, 2009.

with 90% of White students. This represents a 30% difference between White and Black students. It is not surprising that these same three ethnic groups show the lowest levels of academic attainment at every subsequent grade level - whether in elementary, middle, or high school.

It is worth noting that kindergarten school readiness of African-American students is substantially greater than third grade reading achievement for African-American students. While 69% of African-American students enter Minneapolis Public Schools ready for kindergarten, in the third grade only 44% are proficient in reading - a 72% difference.[149] While the data being compared does not track the same cohort of students, the difference is still noteworthy. What accounts for this difference? Some people often blame the lack of parent involvement for the poor academic success of African-American students, but that argument runs contrary to logic. If two-thirds of African-American students enter kindergarten ready, one would expect that the third grade reading would be comparable.

## Minneapolis Public Schools - 3rd Grade Reading Proficiency by Ethnicity (English Proficiency Students)

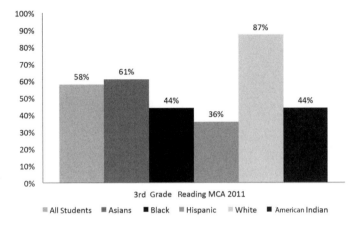

Figure 15. 3rd Grade Reading Proficiency by Ethnicity, Minneapolis
Public Schools, 2010.

This difference between kindergarten readiness and third grade reading is due in large part to the Belief Gap of parents, students, and teachers. Part of this Belief Gap—to be discussed at length in Chapter 5—is that low-income and African-American students do not have the same ability to achieve the level of academic success as their counterparts. Why is this? One of the reasons is that because some African-American parents, who themselves failed in school, have no reason to believe that their children will do any better. In addition, the Teaching Gap —which will also be discussed at length in Chapter 5— places the least experienced teachers in low-income schools with the highest rate of teacher turnover, who are teaching outside their subject matter expertise. This trifecta has proven devastating to the academic outcomes of students in these schools. In almost every other industry except teaching, businesses place their most highly skilled employees on the most difficult problems. This only makes sense. In our current education system, just the opposite is true.

According to 2009 data released by the National Assessment of Educational Progress (NAEP), Minnesota had the highest Black/White achievement gap for 4th grade readers of any state in the country; and it had the 5th highest achievement gap for 8th grade readers of all states in the country.

The epicenter of this local and statewide disaster is in north Minneapolis, where almost 90% of the elementary schools did not make adequate yearly progress (AYP) in 2010 under the NCLB standards. The U.S. Department of Education has labeled a quarter of the elementary and middle schools in north Minneapolis as "chronically underperforming." The situation under NCLB is so bad that in 2012, the Minnesota Department of Education sought and obtained a waiver from the federal AYP requirements.

The Quality Review Report of North Community High School (North) conducted by Minneapolis Public Schools in 2009 found that enrollment in the high school, two-thirds of which was African-American, had dropped from 950 students in 2006-2007 to just 506 students in 2008-2009 (an 88% decline).[149] By the 2010-2011 school year, North had fewer than 200 students (a 475% decline since 2006-2007).[149] Concurrent with the decline in student enrollment, was a precipitous decline in academic achievement. On the 2005 Minnesota Comprehensive Assessment (MCA), North students scored 69% in Reading and 67% in Math—below the statewide average, but not far below. Just two years later, the 2007 scores were 28% and 8%, respectively.

When the Minneapolis Public Schools Superintendent, Bernadeia Johnson, an African-American, proposed closing North in 2010 due to declining enrollment and poor academic performance, the teachers union joined parents and community supporters of North to protest its closure. The teachers union developed a public media campaign touting its support of parents in keeping the school open, but nowhere in this campaign did it ever mention that the school, and by extension its teachers, was failing the children.

Most of Harvest Prep's and Best's students live in north Minneapolis, in the heart of this disaster area, and 91% of its students qualify for free or reduced lunch—a present-day euphemism for children who are poor. Despite the fact that their students have the highest risk of academic failure, over the past two years they have outperformed all other ethnic groups in the city of Minneapolis, including White students, in math as well as in measures of academic growth.

Some critics of Harvest Prep and Best Academy, most of whom see these schools as a threat to their hegemony over the education of low-income students of color, have openly stated or implicitly suggested that Harvest Prep and Best Academy "cherry pick" their students. They argue that this is how Harvest Prep and Best have achieved superior academic results with the same cohort of students as the other public schools in north Minneapolis. In fact, Harvest Prep and Best have a higher percentage of low-income students than more than 90% of the public schools in the Minneapolis and St. Paul metropolitan area, and a higher concentration of African-American students of any school in the entire state. "If we're cherry picking," said Eric Mahmoud jokingly, I'm going to fire the person who's doing the picking." His schools are mandated by state law to accept all students in the order in which they apply. They have the same cohort of students who are physically, emotionally, and sexually abused as students in the public schools. Each year they lose 15-20% of their students due to high mobility and transiency. But regardless of these challenges, there are no excuses for failing to educate the children.

### Harvest Prep's Success

From the very beginning, Harvest Prep has focused on teaching fundamental skills in reading and math, while engaging parents in their children's learning, cultural knowledge, and pride.

Figure 16 shows the combined percentage of students at Harvest Prep, in grades 3 through 6, who were proficient in both reading and math in 2012, compared to the statewide average and the African-American statewide average in Minnesota. In 2012 Harvest Prep exceeded the statewide average by 5% in reading and an astounding 31% in math.[149] When compared to the statewide African-American student performance, Harvest Prep's results were 51% higher in reading, and a mind-boggling 145% higher in math.[149]

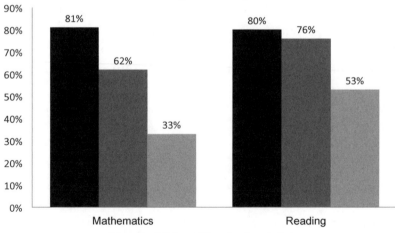

Figure 16. Harvest Prep School 2012 MCA II/III Comparison with All Students in the State and African-American Students in the State

Because the achievement gap is usually measured by how African-American student performance compares to that of White students and other ethnic groups, Figure 17 shows that in 2012 Harvest Prep students were in a statistical dead heat with White students in reading, but outperformed White students by 19% in math.[149]

**Harvest Prep School MCA II/III Comparison of Averages Between White Students and African-American Students in the State Math and Reading Proficiency Scores**

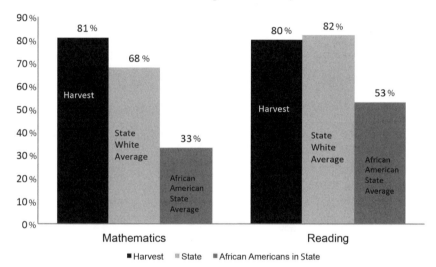

Figure 17. Harvest Prep School 2012 MCA II/III Comparison with State White Average and African-Americans in the State, Math and Reading Proficiency Scores

Figure 18 compares the 2012 math performance of Harvest Prep 3rd through 6th grade students in comparison to the statewide average and the Black statewide average. Harvest Prep outperformed the statewide average in all these grades, and in 5th grade it outperformed the statewide average by an incredible 46%.[149] The difference in performance of African-Americans at Harvest Prep and African-Americans statewide is even more dramatic. From 3rd through 6th grade, Harvest Prep outperformed African-Americans around the state anywhere from 65% to 170% in math.[149]

### Harvest Prep School 2012 MCA II/III Comparison with State Average and Black State Average at Each Grade Level - Math

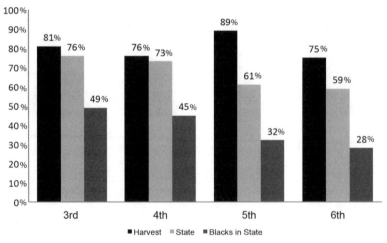

Figure 18. Harvest Prep School 2012 MCA II/III Comparison with State Average and Black State Average at Each Grade Level, Math.

Figure 19 compares the 2012 reading performance of Harvest Prep at every grade level, from 3rd through 6th grade, to the statewide average for all students and the statewide average for Black students. In 3rd and 6th grade, Harvest Prep student performance was in a statistical dead heat at every grade level, except 5th grade, in which it outperformed the statewide average by 9%. Harvest Prep outperformed the statewide Black average from 34% to 49% in 3rd through 6th grade.[149]

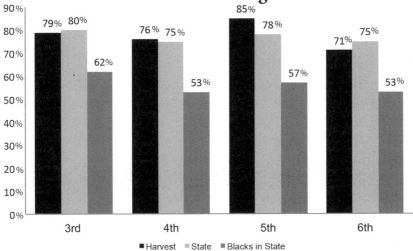

Figure 19. Harvest Prep School 2012 MCA II/III Comparison with State Average and Black State Average at Each Grade Level, Reading.

Figure 20 shows the trend analysis for Harvest Prep's reading test results over the past four years, demonstrating a steady 51% increase.[149] This is an indication that not only are the students getting better, but the system of education at Harvest Prep is getting better. While the achievement gap in reading was reduced between all students in the state and African-American students, going from 26 percentage points to 23 percentage points in reading, Harvest Prep totally eliminated the achievement gap; and, in fact, it reversed the gap in reading in 2012 by going from 53% in 2009 to 80% in 2012. The rise in Harvest Prep reading scores represents a 51% increase in test scores from 2009 to 2012, compared to a corresponding 4% rise in the statewide average over the same time period.[149]

## Harvest MCA Trend Data in Reading, 3rd - 6th Grade

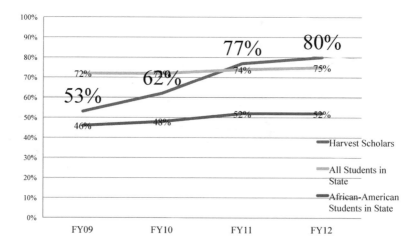

Figure 20. Harvest MCA Trend Data in Reading, 3rd - 6th Grade, 2009–2012

Figure 21 shows the dramatic increase made by Harvest Prep in math over the same three-year period, 2009 to 2012. In 2009, only 43% of Harvest Prep students were proficient in math. But in the ensuing three-year period, Harvest Prep improved from 62% in 2010, to an astounding 82% in 2011, and held steady at 81% in 2012. These results represent an 88% increase in student performance over a 3-year period.[149]

## Harvest MCA Trend Data in Mathematics
## 3rd - 6th Grade

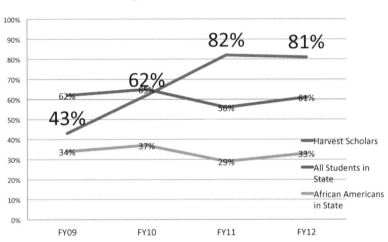

Figure 21. Harvest MCA Trend Data in Mathematics, 3rd - 6th Grade, 2009-2012.

What happened during this three-year period to drive these kinds of results? The answer starts with the following statement of school founder, Eric Mahmoud: "Even though in 2009 Harvest Prep was outperforming all other school districts in Minnesota for African-American children, we were not satisfied with being the highest performing school for African-Americans. We wanted to be the highest performing school in Minnesota - period."

Consequently, during the 2008-2009 school year, the leaders of Harvest Prep set out to visit as many high-performing schools as possible, schools such as Achievement First in New York City, Excellence Charter School for Boys in Bedford-Stuyvesant (New York City), KIPP (Knowledge is Power Program) Affinity in New York City, and Roxbury Preparatory School in Boston, Massachusetts. They learned that every one of these schools ascribed to the following practices: a coherent instructional philosophy, a culture of high expectation and achievement, a rigorous curriculum, data-driven instruction, continuous formative assessments, frequent informal observations of teacher performance, targeted student support and intervention, reading and writing across curriculum, teaching to the whole child, and professional development training. All of them had excellent teachers and school leaders to implement these practices. Each of these practices will be discussed in detail in Chapters 6 and 7.

The reason for the newfound success of Harvest Prep lies in the educational philosophy that Dana Lehman, School Leader at Roxbury Prep, first introduced to Harvest Prep leaders and implemented in 2009; a philosophy that required an answer to three essential questions:

1. What do students need to know and be able to do?
2. How do we teach what they need to know?
3. How do we know that they've gotten it?

Later, in 2011, after reading Richard Dufour's book *Learning by Doing*,[138] two additional questions were added:

4. What do we do if they don't get it the first time the material is taught?
5. What do we do if they already know the material?

The question then became how to implement this philosophy. Harvest Prep leaders decided that they were going to implement the same successful strategies used by the high-performing schools they had visited. As will be discussed in Chapter 6, "How We Get It Done," the strategies involved longer school days and a longer school year, reliance on data to drive instruction, continuous (formative) student assessments, coaching teachers to improve their instruction, and a collaborative approach to planning and assessment. To allocate more time for professional development and data analysis, Harvest restructured its calendar. Friday, which became an early release day for students, was used by teachers and administrators to conduct professional development and data analysis on student performance. By implementing this series of strategies and approaches, Harvest began experiencing the dramatic growth shown in these charts and figures.

An additional psychological and "belief" motivation of the Harvest leaders occurred in 2008-2009, with the election of President Barack Obama and the opportunity to take a group of students to attend the inauguration of President Obama in Washington, D.C. in January 2009.

When President Obama, the first African-American President of the United States of America, was inaugurated on January 20, 2009, Harvest Prep and Best Academy took 25 of its students to witness the historic event. For both the students and their leader, Eric Mahmoud, it was a life-changing event. "President Obama," he said, "forever changed the narrative of what was possible." Shivering on the Mall in Washington, D.C., among hundreds of thousands of jubilant citizens in the bone-chilling cold of that Inauguration Day, January 20, 2009, he vowed to himself that he would spend the rest of his life developing institutions that produced more Americans like Barack and Michelle Obama.

# 4

# Black Boys – An Endangered Species

*We are the best; not because we say it, but because the best is what we do!*

—*Best Academy Creed*

**Case Study 4: Jameer**

Jameer is one of the most amazing young men to have matriculated at Harvest Prep and Best Academy. Academically he had always excelled, but what distinguished Jameer from his peers was his exceptional leadership ability and the depth and breadth of his knowledge of African history and culture. As a fifth grader, Jameer organized his classmates to become "reading buddies" to kindergarten and first-grade students at Harvest Prep and Best Academy. In the 7th grade he was elected student body vice president and then president.

Jameer was one of the 25 students who made the once-in-a-lifetime trip from Minneapolis to Washington, D.C. to witness the inauguration of President Barack Obama. The tour bus quickly turned into a mobile classroom, with students discussing and debating politics, history, and human rights. Although the youngest student on the bus, Jameer was not only leading the discussions, but he was also clearly their thought leader. At times his arguments were more persuasive than those of the teachers and administrators on the bus. Jameer was much more than a high academic achiever; at age 12 he was an exceptional leader.

Every day Best Academy has a community meeting with its 150 middle-school boys. They use part of the time to recognize the achievements of their peers by giving them a "shout-out." But on this day, instead of a shout-out Jameer wanted to give his classmate Jared a "reboot" to recognize the great job he'd done the year before, to acknowledge that he'd had less success this year, and to exhort him not to let his potential go to waste. Jameer's plea was motivating, encouraging, and uplifting. To encourage a classmate before 150 peers; to take the opportunity to encourage Jared publicly in the manner in which Jameer did demonstrated maturity beyond his years. Jameer did not know how Jared would react, but in the spirit of leadership, he took the risk and, as usual, set an example and a standard for others to follow.

## Rationale for a Boys-Focused Program

In an October 25, 2011 interview with Katherine Kersten, a conservative columnist for the *StarTribune*, Eric Mahmoud said, "Best Academy has the highest proportion of African-American boys of any institution in Minnesota. The only institution that competes with us for enrollment of Black boys is the prison system." While made tongue-in-cheek, this statement was meant to emphasize the all too prevalent pipeline-to-prison scenario that has been created for young Black boys.

Much has been researched and written about the epidemic of educational failure among African-American boys. A 2010 report, published by the Council on Great City Schools, stated that less than 12% of African-American boys, nationally, were proficient in reading and math in 4th and 8th grades. In Minnesota, a state nationally recognized for its educational leadership, only 47% of 4th grade and 44% of African American 8th-grade boys were proficient in reading that year.

According to the Kirwan Institute for the Study of Race and Ethnicity at Ohio State University, over the last two decades the nation's leading philanthropic foundations have launched Black male achievement studies and campaigns in response to the worsening statistics about the extreme isolation and negative life outcomes of Black men and boys.[42] The Schott Foundation for Public Education began to issue its "State Report Cards" after concluding that the educational experiences of Black males in the United States constituted a national crisis. During roughly the same period, state and federal authorities established commissions and task forces to study the economic, political, social, and educational exclusion of Black men and boys from the American mainstream.[43]

The depth of this crisis, particularly for Black boys, is perhaps best revealed by the 2010 finding that, for the past 20 years, the average African-American male had performed below the Basic level in every grade and every subject on the National Assessment of Education Progress (NAEP).[44]

In 2007-08, fewer than half of all Black males graduated with their high school cohort. Black boys who fail to complete high school often resurface in the criminal justice system. The 2007 report from the National Council on Crime and Delinquency (NCCD) showed that while Black youth make up about just 16% of the nation's youth population, they account for 30% of juvenile court referrals, 38% of youth in juvenile facilities, and 58% of youth in adult prison. To be sure, a portion of these disparities is attributable to racism, but education is undeniably the most prevalent factor. The 2005 Sentencing Project report, which calculated state rates of incarceration by race and ethnicity, found that Black boys are incarcerated at six times the rate of White youth,[45] while Latino youth are incarcerated at double the rate of White youth.

In the absence of effective policy interventions to disrupt such patterns, the Bureau of Justice Statistics estimated in 1997 that one in every four Black men could expect to spend some time in prison during his lifetime. By 2005 the estimate was one in three.[46]

### The Day it All Came into Focus

In August 2005 Eric Mahmoud was in his hometown of Philadelphia when he began experiencing extreme abdominal pain. Although advised not to travel, he headed back to Minneapolis and school. When his wife picked him up from the airport, she said he looked like a ghost. Within a day he could not walk or talk. Initially misdiagnosed with an enlarged prostate, he had to be rushed to a hospital emergency room a day later. When he arrived his kidneys were functioning at such a low capacity that doctors could not perform diagnostic testing to determine the source of the problem. After nine days his kidney function had improved enough that he could handle a barium solution and have a CT scan of his abdomen. The CT scan revealed that his appendix had ruptured and was spewing toxins into his abdominal cavity. His doctors told him that, miraculously, his body had formed a protective barrier within his abdomen to wall off and protect the rest of his body. Surgery was required to remove the poisonous appendix. During surgery the doctors discovered a cancerous tumor on his small intestine. Had it not been discovered, eventually it would have traveled to his liver and metastasized. At that point he would have developed liver cancer and in all likelihood died from this deadly disease.

In the wake of this life-changing event, Eric took inventory of his life and created a bucket list. One of the things he noted was to develop the best schools in the state of Minnesota. Anyone who has worked with Eric knows how driven he is to achieve excellence for economically and socially disadvantaged children. The hours he puts in, along with the energy and focus he contributes, are herculean. On many days, he is either at school or working on school-related endeavors until midnight. At 4:30 a.m. he wakes up and starts again.

After making a full recovery from the ruptured appendix in 2006, the principal at Harvest Prep, Dr. Callie Lalugba, asked him, "Are you noticing what is happening with our boys?" Intuitively he knew that the boys were having challenges, both academically and behaviorally, but he had not looked at how the boys were doing compared to the girls. What he discovered was that, on average, the girls at Harvest Prep were at least one grade level ahead of the boys in reading and math. The boys outperformed the girls only in suspensions.

While visiting a neighborhood bookstore in Philadelphia in 2006, he came upon Dr. Jawanzaa Kunjufu's book, *Keeping Black Boys Out of Special Education*. The book confirmed what Mahmoud instinctively knew: There are distinct differences in learning styles between boys and girls.

At that point he decided to start an academy focused on instruction for boys. He told his staff in 2006 that Harvest Prep would be known as the most effective school in Minnesota in educating all children—African-American boys in particular. Mahmoud drew an analogy between starting the boys-focused academy to his own life-threatening hospital experience: "The more serious the problem, the more specialized the skills that are needed to solve the problem." Just as his surgery had required five specialists, including those that specialized in nephrology (kidney) and oncology (cancer); African-American boys would require a specialist in the area of education. Mahmoud was fortunate to have on his teaching staff, Ms. Fatou Diahame, who had the skills necessary to put his theory to the test. What started out as an experiment in 2006 with 20 first grade boys became known as Best Academy in 2008, with 200 boys, grades K through 8.

Drawing from his engineering background in the development of a new product, Eric began building a prototype for the education of high-achieving African-American boys in Minneapolis—something that had never been done. Long hours were required, not only of himself, but of his teachers and administrators. Everyone was informed of the plan, which included a 35% increase in in-class time for students. Not everyone was pleased. One of the consequences of this new prototype for education for high-achieving children was that its teachers, who were used to 16 weeks of vacation, a week of personal time off and another week of paid holidays, now had to accept only 10 weeks of vacation, with one week of PTO and one week of holidays. Teachers and administrators were given the option of leaving. While some did leave most stayed. For those who stayed, the effort became a labor of love. Within two years, the prototype was ready for testing, and it proved successful; however, it had to continue to pass the test each year.

The critics complained: "Yes, they're achieving outstanding student outcomes, but teacher turnover is high." However, these critics fail to mention that according to the National Commission on Teaching and America's Future, almost half of all teachers leave the field after just five years.[47] Research shows that in elementary and low-income urban schools, the turnover rate is even higher.[48]

Eric Mahmoud answered critics with another medical analogy: When a patient is dying on the surgical table—much like low-income and African-American children in our educational system—the primary concern is patient survival. The doctors, nurses, and operating room technicians throw the clock out the window; they do what is necessary to save the patient. Similarly, once the education of low-income, African-American and other educationally disadvantaged children have survived the surgery, perhaps schools can go back to business as usual.

## The Effect of the Absence of Male Role Models

According to research data, the physical absence of fathers affects more than 25 million children in the United States. This takes a toll. In a longitudinal study of 1,197 fourth-grade students, researchers observed "greater levels of aggression in boys from mother-only households than from boys in mother-father households."[49] Similarly, children who exhibited violent behavior at school were 11 times as likely to live in families without fathers and six times as likely to have parents who were not married.[50] Teenage boys from disrupted families are not only more likely to be incarcerated compared to boys from intact, two-parent families, but they are also more likely to manifest worse conduct while incarcerated.[51] In north Minneapolis, where Best Academy is located, more than half of the children grow up in fatherless households. This is especially devastating to African-American boys in the Minneapolis Public Schools district, whose gender and ethnic group have had the most academic challenges of all. On every academic measure, African-American boys are losing ground. In 2010 not one African American boy attending North Community High School was considered proficient in both reading and math.

## The Babas Social Fathers Program

In response to the high degree of absent fathers, Best Academy developed the Babas Social Fathers program. The word *baba* is commonly used in African and other cultures to refer to a father, grandfather, or father-like figure in the immediate or extended family. The Babas Social Fathers program consists of men from the community who are like fathers to the boys. These related or unrelated men regularly attend classes to help support and mentor the boys. They also interact with them in social settings. In 2010 one of the social fathers took a group of 8th grade boys on a summer tour. The purpose of the trip was to allow them to have experiences they might not otherwise have. They visited Mt. Rushmore, the Air Force

Academy, the Grand Canyon, Arizona State University, the University of Texas - El Paso, the Alamo in San Antonio, and the Dallas Cowboys stadium. Between sites the boys would work on math problems and reading exercises on their computers, read books, and watch movies with an educational theme—all in a mobile classroom with laptop computers and Wi-Fi (donated by General Mills, Inc.).

The idea for the Babas Social Fathers program came from a conference attended by Mahmoud in 2006 conducted by the Gurian Institute.[52] At the end of the conference, Mahmoud saw a powerful and illustrative documentary produced by "60 Minutes" called *The Delinquents*. It was based on a true story about a herd of elephants that were being moved from one end of South Africa to another. Because there was not enough room in the trucks to transport the adult male elephants, the government veterinarians decided to exterminate them. They then loaded all of the baby elephants into the trucks and moved them to the other end of South Africa. Fifteen years later a large number of rhinoceros were found dead in the area where the baby elephants had been relocated. After investigation it was determined that these now juvenile elephants were guilty of the killings.

The government veterinarians realized that they had made a mistake. In killing the adult males, they had destroyed all male role models. To fix the problem, they found a herd of adult male elephants and transported them to the area where the juveniles had been relocated. Over the next year, not one rhinoceros had been killed. The influence of these male role models had a lasting effect. The conclusion was that the adult males had provided the proper example of male conduct.

After returning home Mahmoud met with Dr. Verna Price, Executive Director of Girls in Action, a Minneapolis-based program designed to mentor, support, and inspire socially- and economically-disadvantaged girls. He told Dr. Price about *The Delinquents*. She explained that in sociology circles the adult male elephant joining the herd of delinquent elephants is called "social fathering." From that conversation developed the Babas Social Fathers program at Harvest Prep and Best Academy. The program, now called Babas and Mamas, is for both boys and girls. It enlists men and women with a commitment to children to work with the boys and girls at Harvest Prep and Best Academy to give them the positive role model they might not otherwise have.

### The Boys' Dramatic Turnaround

Even though Best Academy is less than four years old, it has demonstrated dramatic success with its males—most of whom are African or African-American. After just two years, in 2010, Best's males were outperforming public schools in Minneapolis, St. Paul, and surrounding suburbs—in the statewide average—in math. In reading the males exceeded public schools in Minneapolis and St. Paul, and were just slightly below the statewide average. By the end of its third year, 2011, Best Academy was breaking down all the myths about African-American male inferiority, when 85% of its males, grades 3-8, were shown to be proficient in reading compared to 75% of males statewide, 77% of White males, and 48% of African-American males statewide. In math, 80% of Best's males, grades 3-8, were proficient, compared to 65% of males statewide, 65% of White males, and 30% of African-American males statewide. The males at Best had exceeded the statewide average and White male average by almost 30%.[149] In just two years, reading scores at Best Academy had increased by almost 60%—from 50% in 2009 to 85% in 2011. The results were nothing short of phenomenal.[149]

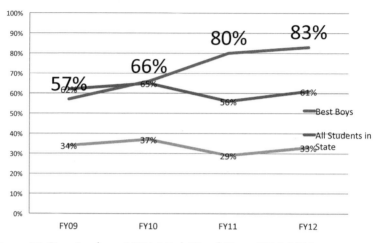

Figure 22. Best Academy MCA Math Trend Data, 2009-2012.

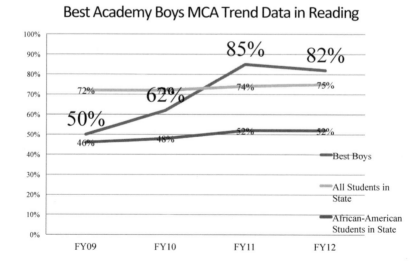

Figure 23. Best Academy, MCA Reading Trend Data, 2009-2012

According to Schooldigger.com, in 2011 Best Academy 3rd grade boys ranked first in the state in math with 100% proficiency, and Best Academy 8th grade boys ranked first in reading. While statewide averages have remained stagnant in reading and have declined in math over the past three years, the test scores of Harvest and Best Academy students have soared. In April 2013 Best Academy was honored by the Coalition of Schools Educating Boys of Color (COSEBOC) as one of five recipients of its National School Award, signifying the highest performing schools in the country for the education of boys of color.

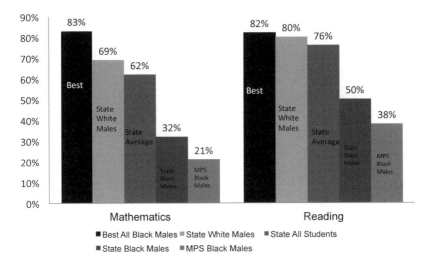

Figure 24. Best Academy, Grades 3-8, MCA II/III Comparison with State White Males, State All Students, State Black Males, and MPS Black Males, 2012.

While the Best Academy boys were excelling, so were the girls at Sister Academy. In the 5th through 8th grades, the girls exceeded statewide averages in math and were just slightly below statewide averages in reading.

**Sister Academy Grades 5-8 MCA II/III
Comparison to Statewide Average
Mathematics and Reading**

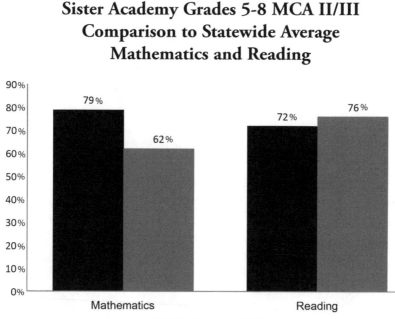

Figure 25. Sister Academy, Grades 5-8, MCA II/III Comparison to Statewide Average, 2012

When compared with the seven public schools in the north side geographic area that are contiguous to Harvest Prep and Best Academy, the contrast is even greater. These seven public schools have combined student populations five times greater than Harvest Prep and Best Academy, yet Harvest Prep and Best Academy produced more students who were proficient in math than all of these seven schools combined. When the data is disaggregated for African-American students in these seven schools, only 13% were proficient in math compared to 80% of the students at Harvest Prep and Best Academy.[53]

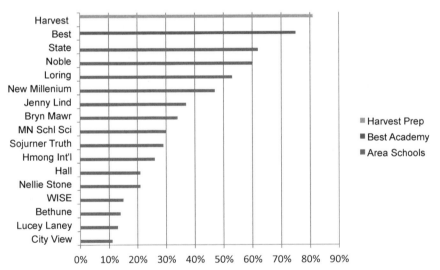

Figure 26. MPS and Charter Schools Serving North Minneapolis K-8, MCA III Math, 2011-2012.

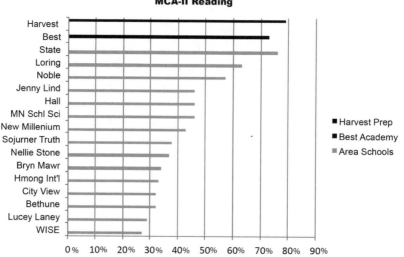

Figure 27. MPS and Charter Schools Serving North Minneapolis K-8,
MCA III, Reading, 2011-2012.

Figure 28 illustrates the performance of Best Academy's East
African ELL program, Best East, where student gains in 2012
paralleled those of the Harvest, Best, and Sister programs. While its
scores are slightly below those of Harvest, Best, and Sister programs
for the period 2011–2012, the Best East program made a dramatic
118% increase in math—exceeding the statewide average by 19%—
and a 26% increase in reading for a program that has only been in
existence for three years.[149]

**Best Academy East, Grades 3-8, MCA II/III Comparison with Statewide Average**

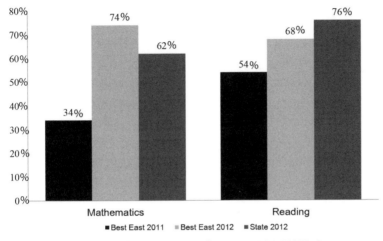

Figure 28. Best Academy East, Grades 3-8, MCA II/III Comparison with Statewide Average.

The research and data is clear: Black boys are an educationally endangered species. In Minnesota only 50% of Black boys in grade 3–8 read at grade level, and only 32% are at grade level in math. Nationally the data is much worse. Notwithstanding the success achieved by the Harvest Prep co-ed program, Eric Mahmoud recognized that the boys were lagging a full grade level behind the girls. In researching the issue, he learned that boys have distinctly different learning styles from that of girls. He determined that specialized attention would have to be given to boys. Beginning with a small prototype class of all boys in 2008, Mahmoud created the boys-focused program called Best Academy. In the space of three short years, Best Academy not only closed, but also reversed the academic achievement gap for Black boys, culminating in the 2013 COSEBOC recognition as one of the five outstanding programs in the entire country for educating boys of color.

# 5

# The "5 Gaps" Framework of Analysis

*The difference between a thermometer and a thermostat is that one tells you the temperature, and the other allows you to adjust the temperature to your needs.*
                              —*Rev. Dr. Martin Luther King, Jr.*

**Case Study 5: Jason**

Jason came to Best Academy as a 6th grader, challenged by some very difficult circumstances. His family, which consisted of his mother and siblings, lived in a homeless shelter. He had never known his father, much less received any support from him. Although Jason was a bright young man and clearly had a great deal of potential, it was hard to see it by his grades and his disruptive behavior. But educators must understand that a student's behavior is often an unconscious response to difficult family circumstances; few know what it is like to be homeless or without food or money. Children internalize these conditions, which then can manifest in their attitude and behavior.

In the first month of Jason's first year at Best Academy, he threw a football at the back of his teacher's head and hit him, which resulted in suspension from school for this dangerous and disrespectful behavior. But just suspending him was not enough to change the behavior of this troubled preteen.

For the rest of that first year Jason struggled. He barely made it through the 6th grade. At the start of 7th grade he continued to struggle with the rules and regimen of Best Academy. By October, Jason wanted out of Best Academy. His mother accommodated his demands and transferred him to another school.

At the start of his 8th grade year, Jason showed up on the doorsteps of Best Academy begging to come back. No one knew what Jason had gone through, but his soiled clothes and the desperation on his face said he was in trouble. Jason knew he was in trouble and was looking to Best Academy to help save him.

Best Academy let him back in, and Jason became the perfect scholar. He exceeded state standards for 8th grade on the MCA tests in both reading and math, and concluded the year with an incredible graduation speech in which he thanked his Best Academy teachers and staff for all that they had done for him. He said he had plans to be an honor student in high school and to graduate from college with a degree in engineering.

Mr. Mahmoud saw Jason the next year, after he had left Best Academy, and the first thing Jason said to him was, "Mr. Mahmoud! I have a 3.5 GPA, and I intend on keeping it at that level all the way through college!" At that point it was clear to Mr. Mahmoud that Best Academy had saved this young man's life.

### The Progenitor

The "5 Gaps" framework of analysis of the achievement gap was created and developed by Eric Mahmoud based on more than 25 years of educational research, training, and experience working with primarily low-income African-American children.

The "5 Gaps" framework is based on the premise that, in order to close the achievement gap, five critical factors must be addressed. These factors are those things over which schools have control. Three often cited reasons for the failure of the public education system for educationally disadvantaged students are these: The children come from poor or low-income families; their parents don't read to the kids; and they don't support their children's learning. While some or all of these *excuses* might be true, the responsibility to educate these children remains. As long as the means to do so is within our control, we must do so by whatever means necessary. Harvest Prep and Best Academy have found and demonstrated a way to do that, despite all of the excuses for why it can't be done.

## The Preparation Gap

### The "Matthew Principle"[54]

*For unto everyone that hath shall be given, and he shall have abundance; but from him that hath not shall be taken away even that which he hath.*
                                        *Matthew 25:29 (KJV).*

This verse from the Bible describes the condition faced by many socially and economically disadvantaged children, regardless of race or ethnicity. In other words, the academically rich get richer, and the academically poor get poorer still. The achievement gap begins early, before the children are old enough to enter school.[55] African-American children enter school behind, and fall further behind, the older they get. According to Dr. Arthur Reynolds, head of the University of Minnesota Institute of Child Development, close to one-half of the achievement gap is present by the time children enter school.[56] Thus, the Preparation Gap identifies the fact that children from certain socioeconomic backgrounds tend to enter school behind their more affluent peers.

In their book, *Meaningful Differences*, Betty Hart and Todd Risley demonstrated that much of the achievement gap that starts early in a child's development is a result of differences in the vocabulary that the primary caregiver, typically the mother, transfers to the child.[57] On average, mothers with a higher education level perform jobs that require them to communicate more and thus will naturally transfer vocabulary to their children at a higher rate than their less educated and economically disadvantaged counterparts. Hart and Risley showed that children of upper-income families have heard 30 million words by age 3 compared with 10 million words heard by children of low-income families.[58] They also found that by age 3, upper-income children have heard 500,000 words of encouragement and 80,000 words of discouragement. Conversely, in the low-income home, the ratio was reversed – by age 3 low-income children had only heard 80,000 words of encouragement, compared to 200,000 words of discouragement. They found a 700-word gap in vocabulary between low-income children and the upper-income children at age 3. They also showed that each year the gap increases.

The Spring 2005 issue of *The Future of Children* confirms the Hart and Risley's study, and identified key social factors in the achievement gap that develop between White and Black children before they even reach kindergarten. The report estimated how much of the gap in school readiness might be explained by each factor:

- Parenting (talking and reading to child, nurturance, and discipline): 25-50% of the Black-White gap
- Child's health: 13% of the Black-White gap
- Maternal breast feeding: 6% of the Black-White gap
- Maternal depression: 6% of the Black-White gap
- Improving the quality of Head Start programs: 4-10% of the Black-White gap
- Low birth weight: 4% of the Black-White gap

In addition to a concentrated effort on early childhood education, prenatal care, and family support, children who are likely to come to school behind must receive some education and training before they enter kindergarten.

The 2010 *Minnesota School Readiness Study* conducted by the Human Capital Research Collaborative for The Minneapolis Foundation[59] stated that children from socially and economically disadvantaged backgrounds (a) are less likely to be fully prepared for kindergarten than their more advantaged peers, (b) and, that their proficiency on entering kindergarten predicts their achievement at third grade, especially in reading and math (as measured by the MCAs). In that study 40% of Minnesota children entering kindergarten did not reach the 75% achievement level for overall school readiness; the largest readiness deficits showed up among students of color.

In Minneapolis a 15-minute standardized assessment of reading and number skills called the Minneapolis Beginning of Kindergarten Assessment (BKA) is given to kindergarten children entering Minneapolis Public Schools. The BKA's total literacy benchmark consists of measures of naming letters and their sounds, rhyming and alliteration, and vocabulary.[60] Overall, 70% of students entering Minneapolis Public Schools are ready for kindergarten, and African-American children are only slightly below that average at 67%. However, the gap between White children and African-American children is a whopping 40% - 94% of White children are ready compared with 67% of African-American children.[149] The gap is even greater for Hispanic and Native American children. But while Hispanic, Native American, and Asian children begin to close the gap by third grade, African-American children fall further behind their White peers. Even among students of color, African-American students face more significant challenges once they start school and the further they advance.

These findings are consistent with a national study of early childhood development conducted by the U.S. Department of Education, first published in 2002. That study, involving 16,000 kindergarten children, found that upper-income students scored 60% above low-income students.[61] These national findings are consistent with a 2003 study, conducted by Wilder Research, of children entering kindergarten in St. Paul, Minnesota. The Wilder study found differences in personal and social development, language and literacy, mathematical thinking, the arts, and physical development, all based on the income and education of the parents.[62] Children in households with lower family income, and children whose parents had less education, tended to have lower school-readiness ratings.[63] The Wilder study also found that 83% of racial/ethnic minority students in St. Paul were from low-income families.[64]

The significance of the 2010 *Minnesota School Readiness Study* and the other studies is that they confirm the preparation gap—and show what can be done to prevent it. Kindergarten students who are prepared and attain proficiency through early childhood education are at least twice as likely to exceed standards on both the MCA reading and math scores in 3rd grade compared to kindergarteners who did not attain overall proficiency. Conversely, kindergarteners that did not attain overall proficiency were more than twice as likely to have been in special education or retained by 3rd grade, even when accounting for gender, race/ethnicity, parent education, or income.

Educators use 3rd grade reading as a benchmark because between kindergarten and 3rd grade children are learning to read. However, beginning in 4th grade they are reading to learn. If students have not acquired basic grade-level reading skills by the 4th grade, they typically struggle with learning both the mechanics of reading and the content of what is read. This is why learning to read by the 3rd grade is so critical. The conclusion is that early childhood education is a vital foundation to future educational growth for children, particularly those from low-income families and from families in which the parents have had less education.

It must be emphasized that the findings from these studies should not be interpreted as assessing the innate ability of the children who were not proficient. What these studies do indicate, however, is that if there is no intervention in the academic development of these students at very early stages, the lack of school readiness is likely to perpetuate itself throughout the student's academic career. More importantly, it tells us that more resources must be invested up front, both human and capital, to prepare disadvantaged students for kindergarten. As Becky Roloff, businesswoman and now CEO of the Minneapolis YWCA told the African-American Leadership Forum Education Work Group in 2010, "In business if 30-40% of our inventory was defective even before production began, there is no way we could expect to stay in business. The failure to prepare children for kindergarten is the same thing."

While longitudinal studies of early childhood programs, such as Head Start, suggest that gains made in early childhood education can fade in the first few years of elementary school,[65] early childhood education remains important. This data simply tells us that we must continue to educate our children after the foundation has been established. More importantly, if they are not adequately prepared when they enter kindergarten they are far less likely to make it to graduation; and as the statistics on the social costs show, children who are inadequately educated are much more likely to end up without a job, on welfare, in poverty, incarcerated—or all of the above. Elementary schools that don't have an early childhood pipeline component to their program must recognize that they will be getting children who come to school behind, before they start kindergarten, and must put resources in place to address the problem. The remaining four gaps that will be discussed in this chapter are solutions to the Preparation Gap.

## The Time Gap

*The key to academic success is great teaching, and more of it.*
—*Chris Barbic*

For students that are behind academically, time is their greatest enemy. Paraphrasing Geoffrey Canada, President and CEO of the dramatically successful Harlem Children Zone, "Simple physics tells us that if African-American children enter kindergarten behind, if they spend the same amount of time on task in school as children who are ahead of them, they'll never catch up."

In order to close the gap for students who are behind, more time must be made available for them to catch up; and more importantly, we must make more effective use of the time we have.

### The Hidden Culprits: Inadequate Classroom Time

Former Minneapolis Public School Superintendent Dr. Carol Johnson, speaking at an Achieve Minneapolis event in November 2011 stated, "In the business world they say 'Time is Money'. In education 'Time is Justice'. Six (6) hours per day is not enough to educate students that are behind. Enough time for some is not enough time for others."[66]

According to Mid-continent Research for Education and Learning (McREL),[67] U.S. schools provide insufficient instructional time for what students need to learn. According to McREL, 200 standards and 3,093 benchmarks are taught in grades K-12, which require 15,465 hours of instruction. The typical school year has 180 days with 5.5 hours of instruction each day for 13 years (K-12). At best that provides only 12,870 hours of instruction, leaving a 2,595 hour deficit between the time needed to learn and the time available to learn.

When the amount of time in school is calibrated to determine the amount of time actually involved in student instruction, the results are even more alarming. An observation of 2,000 classrooms across America conducted by Learning 24/7 found that the actual use of classroom time for instruction varied anywhere from 21% to 69%.[68] At 69%, 12,870 hours of available time is reduced to 8,880 hours, which is less than 60% of the time needed to learn the standards and benchmarks. In schools marked by behavioral issues and other distractions, Learning 24/7 found that actual class time can be as low as 21%. The conclusion is that, at the very best, children in the U.S. are receiving less than 60% of the instructional time needed to learn, and at worst, just a little over 20%. Under even the best of circumstances, 40% of the time needed to learn the established standards and benchmarks must be made up somewhere else – either at home, in after-school tutoring, in summer school, or in a longer school day and school year.

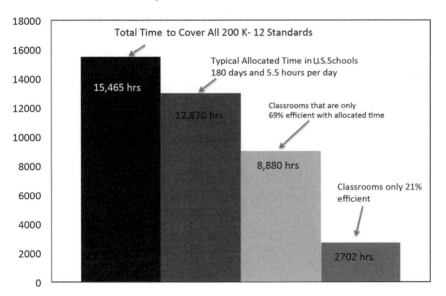

**McRel Study of Time Needed to Cover 200 K – 12 Standards**

Total Time to Cover All 200 K- 12 Standards

15,465 hrs

Typical Allocated Time in U.S. Schools
180 days and 5.5 hours per day

12,870 hrs

Classrooms that are only
69% efficient with allocated time

8,880 hrs

Classrooms only 21%
efficient

2702 hrs

Figure 29. Teaching Time Needed; and Time Available, 2008.

Further compounding the problem, according to McREL, is that in the United States we spend far less time teaching far more topics than countries that outperform us. It's the proverbial "Mile wide and inch deep." For example, in the fourth grade, the United States spends 180 days to teach 78 math topics, whereas Japan spends 253 days teaching 47 topics, and Germany spends 230 days teaching 23 topics. Both countries greatly outperform the U.S. The first difference in these two countries that are outperforming us is that they have far more days in school than we have, amounting to 22–29% more time. The second is that they cover far fewer topics, which allows them to go deeper. According to the National Education Commission on Time and Learning, students abroad are required to work on demanding subject matters at least twice as long as U.S. students.

In a recent conversation with an upper middle-income suburban school parent, Eric Mahmoud learned that the parent was spending $75 per hour for math assistance for their child because the school teacher refused to provide assistance to the child after class hours. The expenditure amounted to $1,000 per month, and this was for a straight A student! This magnifies the point that there is insufficient classroom time. It also highlights the unwillingness of some teachers to put in extra time to teach the subjects children are expected to learn, because it has not been collectively bargained for. Often teachers want to give students the additional help they need and deserve, but union leadership cautions them against doing so, because it's outside of the scope of the collective bargaining agreement. The problem of inadequate classroom time and after-school assistance is magnified for students who are most in need.

### The Summertime Learning Gap

According to recent studies, the problem of inadequate classroom time for instruction is compounded for low-income children—compared with middle- and upper-income children—who lose ground during the summer when they're out of school, and the gap increases every year.[69] Some educational experts refer to this summer-time gap as a part of an "opportunity gap," or more appropriately, a "lack of opportunity" gap. It is estimated by some experts that 65% of the achievement gap is a gap in opportunity.[70] Upper-income families can make up for the gap in learning time in school identified by McRel and the summer-time gap. They can give their children multiple other opportunities to learn simply through conversation at the dinner table, or in the car, or supplemental tutoring and summer activities, or travel opportunities. For example, a young medical school tutor whose parents were chemistry professors at a university discussed the chemical compounds of table salt at breakfast. Consequently, high school and college chemistry was a breeze for that student. Children from families whose parents are professionals are more likely to watch, read, and discuss local, national, and international news regularly in normal conversation. Middle-income families can provide their children with some of these opportunities, for example, by enrolling them in summer math, science, and computer camps. But for families of low-income children, there is little chance to make up this time. A significant number of low-income children spend their summers with educational surrogates like video games, music, or dysfunctional and mind-deadening TV or movies.

In order to close the achievement gap with low-income children, more time and more effective use of time-on-task is needed by extending the school day and the school year, and by making available multiple other opportunities to learn. New Jersey, a state that has substantially closed the high school graduation gap, attributes much of its success to the fact that since 2003 it provided students with more hours of education each day, on weekends, and during the summer. In its 2010 report on Black males, the Schott Foundation, citing New Jersey as an example, identified after-school and summer programming as a "condition for success" in closing the gap.[71]

### What is Instructional Time?

Figure 30 illustrates the use of time available to teach children as a set of concentric circles that surround the core goal of Interactive Instructional Time.

### Instructional Time Model

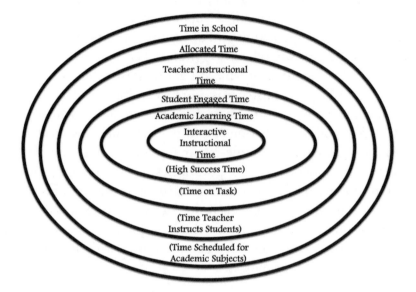

Figure 30. Instructional Time Model, 2008.

Time in School means the school calendar year—the number of days students are in school. Allocated Time, a function of Time in School, represents the number of hours a student is in school each year. Allocated Time is then divided into two categories: Teacher Instructional Time, when the student is in a classroom or instructional environment, and Non-Instructional Time, when the student is in the cafeteria, study hall, passing between classes, etc.[72] Non-Instructional Times are excluded from Teacher Instructional Time because the student is not in a direct learning environment.[73]

From Teacher Instructional Time comes the actual amount of time a student is engaged in learning. This is called Student Engagement Time, Engaged Time, or Time-on-Task—the actual amount of time a student spends each day tending to school-related tasks,[74] such as following directions and engaging in learning activities. Academic Learning Time is then derived from Time-on-Task. It is the ultimate goal of classroom instruction: the amount of time the learner spends actively engaged in worthwhile tasks at a high level of success.[75] The school year must thus be planned to maximize the amount of Academic Learning Time.[76]

### Addressing the Time Gap

Educators and society can no longer be content competing with ourselves. The marketplace for success is now the entire world. To compete with our international counterparts in the global economy, our educational systems need some fixes. That much is clear. It is not too dramatic to say that our survival as a nation depends on whether we have the will to make these changes.

The school day, the number of school days, and the school year must all be extended to allow more time to learn and to reduce the "summertime achievement gap."

Time must be used differently through expanded learning opportunities. In the now famous *90/90/90 Study*, the schools that made the largest gains in reducing the achievement gap made dramatic changes in their schedule.[77] 90/90/90 schools are schools with 90% low-income students and 90% ethnic minorities that achieved 90% proficiency on standardized testing. At the elementary level, they routinely devoted three hours each day to literacy, with two hours of reading and one hour of writing. At the secondary level, they routinely provided double periods of English and math. To break the mold in student achievement, successful schools discovered they had to break the schedule.

# The Teaching Gap

*If the student hasn't learned, the teacher hasn't taught.*
                                        —*Siegfried Engelmann*

## Developing Nation Builders

*[A]fter parents, the biggest impact on a child's success comes from the man or woman at the front of the classroom. In South Korea, teachers are known as "nation builders." Here in America, it's time we treated the people who educate our children with the same level of respect.*
                                — *President Barack Obama*

Research shows that the effects of teaching dwarf all others factors of student learning. Good teachers are the single most important in-school factor that contributes to student success.[78] Good teachers make good schools.[79] Students who get several effective teachers in a row will soar, no matter what their family backgrounds; while students who have even two ineffective teachers in a row rarely recover.[80]

Highly effective teachers are most critical for children at risk, for those furthest behind.[81] Teacher effectiveness is a major factor in a student's academic growth from year to year.[82] In one study, fifth-grade math students in Tennessee who had three consecutive highly effective teachers scored 52–54 percentage points ahead of students who had three consecutive teachers who were least effective, even though both groups had the same achievement rates prior to entering second grade. A similar study in Texas showed a difference of 34 percentage points in reading and 49 percentage points in math.[83]

As mentioned earlier, teachers at Harvest Prep and Best Academy must ask five essential questions:

1. What do my children need to know and be able to do?

2. What are the most effective ways to teach what they need to know?
3. How do we know that they got it?
4. What do we do after they are taught it and didn't get it?
5. What do we do if they already know the material?[84]

Highly qualified teachers must be well trained in content, cognitive strategies, and affective strategies. In working with diverse student populations, teachers need continuous opportunities for growth and improvement in differentiated instruction and formative assessment.

Differentiated instruction means instruction geared to the student's skill level. It presupposes that the skill levels of each student are known, by the students having been given some form of assessment. With this knowledge the teacher will plan lessons that give each student support at her skill level. Students are given a common assignment, but grouped according to their ability. Instruction is then varied based upon each group's skill level.

Formative assessments are an ongoing way of assessing student progress as they are being taught and then making adjustments in instruction based on feedback received from students. For example, after a quiz or test, the teacher will review the results and determine which students understood the material. For those students who did not understand the material, instruction will be adjusted to meet their needs. For more advanced students who understood the material, the teacher looks for material that is more rigorous or challenging. By way of analogy, the gardener will evaluate the garden overall, but at the same time, he will look at individual types of flowers to determine whether they need more or less sun, water, or nutrients.

First and foremost, the school must have a strong focus on teaching and learning. The instructional program must be what a school is all about, driving daily efforts. Professional development for teachers is critical to a strong curriculum and instructional program.[85] Giving teachers a sustained opportunity to improve their classroom skills appears, thus far, to yield the best return for the investment.[86]

### For School Boards and Policy Makers: The Most Effective Teachers Must be Placed Where the Greatest Need Exists

The system by which teachers are allocated to schools needs major changes. As previously stated, students who get several effective teachers in a row will soar, no matter what their family backgrounds, while students who have two ineffective teachers in a row rarely recover.[87] Similarly, students who have three great teachers in a row will produce gains 1.5–2 years ahead of students who have less effective teachers.[88] It is estimated that children with excellent teachers – teachers in the top 25% - make 3 times the progress of students with teachers in the bottom 25%.[89]

Classrooms in low-income and high-minority schools are far more likely than those in high-income and low-minority schools to be in schools with high teacher turnover, teachers with less experience, and teachers teaching out of their field of expertise.[90] Consequently, low-income and African-American children suffer from the trifecta of inexperienced teachers, high teacher turnover, and teachers teaching out of their field of expertise.[91] At present the system rewards teachers financially and professionally primarily for the amount of time they have spent in the profession and for the amount of additional education they have obtained.[92] These same teachers have more say in schools to which they are assigned; and, they are more likely to prefer teaching in middle and upper income schools where there are fewer student behavior issues and the students are more culturally similar to them. As a consequence, the least experienced teachers end up in schools with the most challenges and the fewest resources.

Harvest Prep and Best Academy have achieved success because of the outstanding teaching staff they have been able to assemble. They have been able to attract new teachers who are top graduates in their teaching class, and have retained many of their master teachers. Dr. Lesa Clarkson, Professor of Mathematics at the University of Minnesota, also teaches at Best Academy. Dr. Clarkson has helped devise the math curriculum and instruction at Harvest Prep and Best Academy, which has accounted, in large part, for the outstanding success they have achieved. Ms. Fatou Diahame and Ms. Loretta Hall are long-tenured master teachers. In 2011 Ms. Diahame's 3rd grade boys were 100% proficient in math on statewide MCA testing.

Unfortunately, according to a recent study conducted at Baylor University, state policymakers' attention to teacher quality is highly responsive to low graduation rates among White students, but not to low graduation rates among Black students. The study findings are evidence that "the persisting achievement gap between White and Black students has distinctively political foundations," the researchers wrote.

The article, entitled "The Political Foundations of the Black-White Education Achievement Gap", is published in the journal *American Politics Research*. It is co-authored by Patrick Flavin, Ph.D., an assistant professor of political science in Baylor's College of Arts & Sciences, and Michael Hartney, a Ph.D. candidate at the University of Notre Dame.

The researchers' findings show that inequality persists when it comes to education reform. "Instead of promoting equality of opportunity, America's system of K-12 education -- which relies heavily on state and local control -- may worsen political inequalities," the researchers wrote. "Whether analyzed at the policymaking level or the level of individual citizens' political attitudes, white students receive far more attention and subsequent response compared to African-American students," Flavin said.

The Baylor study findings are consistent with observations of local urban school districts in Minnesota. Despite the fact that local urban school districts have developed mechanisms to determine who their most effective teachers are, little effort has been made to put the most effective teachers where the greatest need exists.

Another systemic problem is that a majority of teachers in Minnesota colleges are not being adequately trained to teach racially and ethnically diverse students. A 2008 study found that, in a large sample of accredited bachelor degree programs, only 43% required at least one course in working with culturally and ethnically diverse children.[93] In an effort to begin to address this issue, the Bush Foundation Teaching Program in Minnesota requires students to co-teach in schools with low-income and ethnically diverse children during their educational training.

### Student Performance Must Be the *Sine Qua Non* of Teaching

Paraphrasing Garrison Keillor's Lake Wobegon soliloquy, "We all have a tendency to think we're above average in all areas, except those in which actual measurement is available." The same holds true for teaching. Most teachers think and believe that they are above average. That is because, until just recently, there were no effective ways to measure whether students were actually learning. To the extent that teachers were evaluated at all, they were evaluated on whether they could check off that they had covered all of the teaching rubrics.

Student performance must be the *sine qua non* of teacher evaluation. *Sine qua non* refers to an indispensable and essential action, condition, or ingredient. Effective schools are characterized by the use of student performance data in decision making and by regular student assessments tied to the curriculum. Teachers must do continuous formative assessment and provide constant feedback that is focused on improving learning. Using a proprietary curriculum, for example, Scott Foresman or Houghton Mifflin, among others, is not sufficient to move students more than one year's growth in an academic year. Frequent assessment of student progress and multiple opportunities for assessment must take place.

There should be clear rewards and consequences for both teachers and leaders for school completion outcomes, but public school teachers, districts, and unions have a strong aversion to holding teachers accountable for student performance. In fact, some school districts are trying to get rid of standardized testing altogether.

It is absurd to think that in today's education system teachers are evaluated without regard for improved student performance. That would be like evaluating a football, basketball, or baseball coach without regard for the team's win/loss record. Yet many Minnesota teachers' unions are intransigent in their opposition to student performance as a means of evaluating teacher effectiveness. School leaders must have the ability to reward teachers who are "beating the odds." Teachers who are "beating the odds" are those teachers who are taking students who are furthest behind academically and moving them farther ahead than their peers who are teaching similarly situated children. As mentioned earlier excellent teachers achieve three times the annual student growth compared to low-performing teachers. School leaders must also have the ability to address teachers who are ineffective. As the movie *Waiting for Superman* so clearly demonstrated in the "Dance of the Lemons," low-performing teachers are passed on from one school to another, and unfortunately, the data shows that they usually end up in schools where the students have the greatest need for excellent – not low performing – teachers. Just as students must be constantly assessed and evaluated, teachers and administrators must be constantly assessed and evaluated. A rigorous process with clear performance goals, supervision and support, and annual performance reviews should be used to select teachers.

### Teachers Must Have Empathy

The following question is often asked of Eric Mahmoud because his student population is predominantly African-American: Do your teachers have to be African-American to teach African-American children? Stated another way: Can White teachers effectively teach African-American children? According to the experience at Harvest Prep and Best Academy, the answer is yes ... maybe. If teachers don't have experience in the background and history of the cultures from which the children come, they must have empathy and must be able to respect the essential humanity and culture of others. It is preferable that they have experience working with ethnically diverse and low-income students and cultures, but is not essential, as long as they have the heart and the mind to learn. It is also preferable that they have consistently and continuously encountered other diverse student populations in their undergraduate licensing process. Student teaching is not enough. At present less than one-half of national teacher training universities require students to take courses in cultural competency.

If teachers come to the profession without this cultural sensitivity or background, they must have empathy for the students being taught – students who often come from families and backgrounds quite different than their own. Understanding these differences must be mainstreamed into the curricula of teacher preparation programs, and it must be measured and evaluated. Cultural content must be linked with subject content. Teachers must strengthen their knowledge, understanding, and use of culturally proficient strategies.

Teachers need to have a deep understanding of effective and varied teaching approaches. Methods that work with some may not work with others. Teachers must be able to adapt and respond in real time to classroom and non-classroom situations. Students need an inclusive curriculum—pluralistic and multicultural. For example, because most students at Harvest Prep and Best Academy are African-American, they are taught African-American history and achievement in addition to American/European history. Images and stories of African-American heroes and historical figures cover the school walls. "Lift Every Voice and Sing"—the African-American national anthem—is taught in addition to the National Anthem. Students are taken on trips to visit historically Black colleges and universities (HBCUs) in addition to local colleges and universities. Some even attended the inauguration of President Obama. It is important that the students see themselves as achievers.

### Alternative Pathways to Becoming Teachers Must be Created

We are confronting a state of emergency in our community. We must be able to draw effective teachers from all quarters—not just from institutions of higher learning, but from working professionals—experts in math, science, English, and technology who have experienced real-life success and can impart that knowledge.

In Minnesota and many other states, there are limited points of entry into the teaching profession. This compounds Minnesota's challenge in attracting high-performing teaching candidates. According to the Itasca Project Report, commissioned by the Minnesota Business Partnership and published in 2009, 99% of Minnesota teachers come through traditional teacher preparation programs.[94] Further compounding the problem is that the majority of students from these programs are from the bottom third of their classes.[95] Alternative pathways that have demonstrated success in other states must be developed. Barriers must be removed that prevent high-achieving college and post-college graduates and professionals who are interested in teaching—but do not have an education degree—from entering teaching. Programs such as Teach for America have demonstrated positive results by placing high-performing college graduates, who may not have a teacher's license, in low-income urban and rural school environments. An "all hands on deck" approach is needed to addressing America's educational problems. It is unfortunate that Minnesota's effort to create alternative teacher certification has fallen victim to politics. After having passed alternative certification legislation in 2011, the teacher certification process has yet to be substantially implemented.

### Traditional Teaching Preparation Must be Transformed

To match the supply and demand, to improve the value proposition of teaching, and to ensure quality, high admission standards must be set and enforced. The preparation curriculum must be evaluated, and the emphasis on the effective use of student data must be increased. Effective schools are characterized by the use of student performance data in decision making and regular student assessments that are tied to the curriculum. Transparency and accountability must be introduced that should be tied to student outcomes in order to drive continuous improvement. There should be clear rewards and consequences for school completion outcomes.

Highly-qualified teachers must be well-trained in content, cognitive strategies, and affective strategies. When working with diverse student populations, teachers need continuous opportunities for growth and to make improvements in differentiated instruction and formative assessments. Professional development for teachers is a critical part of a strong curriculum and instructional program. Giving teachers a sustained opportunity to improve their classroom skills appears, thus far, to yield the best return for the investment. But first and foremost, the school must have a strong focus on teaching and learning. The instructional program must drive daily efforts.

# The Leadership Gap

*At the factory I used to run, if we had a failure rate of 0.005%, we'd shut down the line until we figured out the problem. In our education system we're failing with 40%, 50%, and 60% of our African-American children, but we just keep the line running.*

—*Eric Mahmoud*

The impact of principals and school leaders on student outcomes is second only to that of teachers. Some would argue that it is first. School districts that have been most effective in closing the achievement gap are headed by strong and effective district leaders, including district superintendents and school principals. Such leaders have applied proven models of academic success.

In the famous *90/90/90 Study* and report, the distinguishing feature of the successful schools was not merely that they had standards, but rather how the standards were implemented, monitored, and assessed.[96] One of the most powerful findings of the *90/90/90 Study* was the continuous nature of the success of these schools, even as the poverty of students attending these schools remained intractable from year to year. Moreover, these schools achieved these results without specific programs or proprietary models. The message is special textbooks, curriculum materials, or secret information is not needed to achieve the level of success enjoyed by these schools.[97]

School leaders must understand that they are the instructional and academic leaders of the school, and they must be results-oriented. In the United Kingdom educational leaders have implemented a rigorous inspection and intervention process that not only drives school improvements, but has also seen the number of required interventions drop by over 50% in 10 years.[98]

Leadership must focus on instructional excellence rather than administrative issues. Student outcomes, the ultimate goal of public education, must be linked to major elements of the educational system in ways that facilitate understanding about what is and what is not working.[99]

For managers in fields outside of the education system, results begin with a systematic effort to identify and groom potential leaders. Access to ongoing mentorship and training helps develop the leadership skills demanded of front-line managers. Empowering leaders to choose their staff—and then holding them accountable for its results—produces teams that are focused on commonly shared goals.[100]

Last, but by no means least, leaders in education, business, government, philanthropy, and the community must come together to exercise a Collective Impact across sectors to effect large-scale educational change.[101] The scale and complexity of the U.S. public education system has thwarted attempted reforms for decades. Major funders, such as the Annenberg Foundation, the Ford Foundation, and the Pew Charitable Trust, have abandoned many of their efforts in frustration after acknowledging a lack of progress. After World War II the United States was the global leader with the highest high school graduation rate in the world. Now it ranks 18th among the top 24 industrialized nations, with more than 1 million secondary school students dropping out every year.[102] The heroic efforts of countless teachers, administrators, and nonprofits—together with billions of dollars in charitable contributions—may have led to important improvements in individual schools and classrooms; yet system-wide progress has not been obtained.[103]

**There Must be a "One Table/Collective Impact" Approach to Solve This Problem**

The achievement gap has been studied and discussed ad nauseam, with very little to show for the effort. Notwithstanding the proliferation of research, studies, and theories, only isolated gains have been made in addressing this problem.

At the African-American Leadership Forum - Policy Makers Forum in March 2010, Todd Otis, former Minnesota legislator and current Executive Director of Ready for K, stated that there must be a cross-sector approach to addressing the achievement gap, one that brings together leaders in education, business, government, philanthropy, and the community. Efforts that have proven the most successful in closing the achievement gap and taking it to scale have used this One Table also known as the "Collective Impact" approach, which brings together leaders in each of these sectors and connects the entire educational continuum from "cradle to career."[104] It connects early childhood education to family support systems, to an extended school day and school year, to quality teaching and leadership, and establishes a system of agreed-upon metrics for evaluating success. The acclaimed Harlem Children's Zone in New York is one such model, albeit confined to a limited geographic area. The Northside Achievement Zone, also known as NAZ, under the leadership of Sondra Samuels, is a program in north Minneapolis that was patterned after the Harlem Children's Zone. NAZ employs the collective impact approach, with one of its major focuses being to reduce the educational achievement gap for children in the zone. In December 2011 NAZ received a $28 million Promise Neighborhood award from the federal Department of Education.

Another successful model of this approach is the Strive effort. Originating in Cincinnati, Ohio, Strive brought together cross-sector local leaders to tackle the student achievement crisis and to improve education throughout greater Cincinnati and northern Kentucky. In the four years since the group was launched—and despite the recession and budget cuts—Strive has documented success in 34 of 53 success indicators that track educational improvement. One of these indicators is high school graduation rates, where the achievement gap has been closed.

The Strive effort in Cincinnati has been successful because community leaders decided to abandon their individual agendas in favor of a collective approach to improving student achievement. More than 300 leaders of local government, education, philanthropy, and business united their efforts behind a common systematic effort, with an agreed upon Roadmap for Success from cradle to career. Leaders agreed that it would make little difference to fix one part of the educational continuum without addressing all parts of the continuum at the same time.

Unlike many of its predecessors, Strive didn't try to create a new educational program or attempt to convince donors to spend more money. Instead, through a carefully structured process, Strive focused the entire educational community (including business, philanthropy, and others) on a single set of goals, all measured in the same way.

In order to close the achievement gap on this scale, Minnesota has adopted this collective impact approach in an organizational effort called Generation Next. The recommendation to bring a Strive-like model to Minnesota was the idea of Dr. Robert Jones,[105] former Senior Vice President of Academic Administration at the University of Minnesota and former co-chair of the Education Work Group of the African-American Leadership Forum. The University of Minnesota and the African-American Leadership Forum co-sponsored the initiative that led to the creation of Generation Next. Generation Next has brought together the mayors and school superintendents of Minneapolis and St. Paul, the presidents of the University of Minnesota and Minnesota State Colleges and Universities (MNSCU), together with philanthropic leaders and corporate executives. Modeled after the Strive effort in Cincinnati, Generation Next is designed to identify best practices that would connect early childhood education to family support systems, to an extended school day and school year, to quality teaching and leadership, all with a system of agreed-upon metrics for evaluating success.

### Systematic Efforts Must be Made to Identify and Groom Potential Leaders

As previously stated, a formula with demonstrated results begins with a systematic effort to identify and groom potential leaders. Access to ongoing mentorship and training helps develop the leadership skills demanded of front-line managers. Empowering leaders to choose their staff—and then holding them accountable for its results—produces teams that are focused on commonly shared goals.[106] Programs in Minneapolis, such as the Leadership Academy, Principal's Academy, Achieve Minneapolis, and Lead for Charters have been specifically designed to address this leadership issue in Minneapolis. Achieve Minneapolis, a program funded by General Mills, Inc., Cargill, and Medtronic, was specifically created to identify and develop new school leaders. Additional collaborative efforts are being made to identify emerging school leaders between local public schools and leaders of high performing charter schools that have a history of success with African-American and low-income children.

### School Leaders Must be Evaluated and Must be Able to Choose Their Teachers

Just as teacher accountability is demanded for producing student results, school leaders must undergo similar performance assessments. Principal evaluations should be mandated and conducted by the district superintendent or designee and should use student data to determine a principal's effectiveness.[107] However, to adequately assess school performance, leaders must be empowered to choose their staff.

They must then be held accountable for their results. Research shows that this produces teams that are focused on commonly shared goals.[108]

**Systems of Proven Results Must be Implemented**

According to Eric Mahmoud, leadership is primarily responsible for ensuring that the coherence of the systems, structures, people and culture are all moving toward the academic goal. Harvest Prep and Best Academy have adopted the Public Education Leadership Project (PELP) model of leadership (see Figure 31) developed at Harvard University. Implementation of this model is discussed in Chapter 6.

**The Inner Core**

The inner part of the model is the Instructional Core, which includes three interdependent components: teachers' knowledge and skill, students' engagement in their own learning, and academically challenging content or rigor. All three of these components must be improved to increase student performance.

**The Middle Circle**

Strategy represents a coherent set of actions that a school or school district deliberately undertakes to strengthen the instructional core in order to raise student performance both school and district-wide. Developing coherence among these actions at the district, school, and classroom levels will make a district's chosen strategy more scalable and sustainable.

**The PELP Coherence Framework**

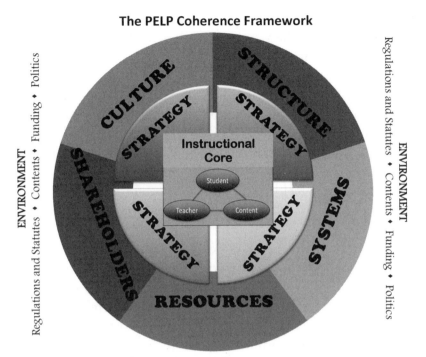

Figure 31. PELP Coherence Framework, 2002.

### The Outer Circle

Stakeholders are the people and groups inside and outside the school district—district and school staff, governing bodies, unions and associations, parents and parent organizations, civic and community leaders, and other organizations.

Culture constitutes the norms, values, and attitudes that define and drive behavior in the district.

Structures help define how the work of the school district gets done. It includes how people are organized, who has responsibility and accountability for results, and who makes or influences decisions. Such structures can be both formal (deliberately established organizational forms) and informal (the way decisions get made or the way people work and interact outside of formal channels).

Systems are managed by school districts using a variety of processes and procedures that get the work done. Systems are built around such important functions as career development and promotion, compensation, student assignment, resource allocation, organizational learning, and measurement and accountability. Most practically, systems help people feel like they do not have to reinvent the wheel when they need to complete an important, and often multistep, task.

Resources concern the management of the flow of financial resources throughout the organization; it includes people and physical assets, such as technology and data. When school districts carefully manage their most valuable resource--people--and understand what investments in technology and data systems are necessary to better support teaching and learning, the entire organization is brought closer to coherence.

Environment includes all of the external factors that can have an impact on strategy, operations, and performance, such as state regulations and statutes, contracts, funding, and politics.

### Creating a Vision for What is Possible

The leader for the gap-closing school or school district must help the staff create a vision of the level of achievement that is possible for the school's students. The saying "seeing is believing" is true. By making study visits to high-performing schools, attending conferences and seminars, and conducting book studies of effective practices in closing the achievement gap, leaders can shape the vision for the teaching staff that is academically possible for all students.

## Being Relentless in the Pursuit of the Possible: The Desire to Become the "Best of the Best"

Being relentless in the pursuit of the possible reflects the school leader's responsibility for continuously improving the instructional school culture, as well as its operational systems, in order to improve student outcomes. For example, three years ago Harvest Prep was what one of its friends and supporters referred to as "The Best of the Worst." In other words their test scores were well above all other schools and school districts for low-income and African-American children: They were the best in that regard. But they were still below the statewide average, and well below the White average in both reading and math: In that regard, they were the worst.

Eric Mahmoud set out with missionary zeal to prove that Harvest Prep and Best Academy could become the "Best of the Best." Over the next three years, the schools engaged in an exhaustive examination of what they were doing internally and compared themselves to what other high-performing schools were doing throughout the country that had closed and, in many cases, reversed the achievement gap. Eric Mahmoud visited high performing, gap-closing schools; he took notes and asked questions. He looked at the systems and data being used to improve student achievement. He observed that some high-performing schools had state of the art technology, while others had bare bones, even Spartan, operations. The common thread was that they all got the job of educating students done.

## Seeking and Developing Skills and Will in Others

It is critical to develop the skills and the will in others to support the vision. Great teachers must have both the skills and the will to impact student achievement. In low-performing schools, in particular, leaders must look for teachers who have a burning desire, a sense of urgency, to make significant changes in student outcomes. Great teachers can see their students' innate abilities to achieve and develop ways to bring them out. Leaders must be clear on what those teaching skills are and constantly seek to develop those skills in all teachers.

## The Belief Gap

*"If you can control a man's thinking you do not have to worry about his action. When you determine what a man shall think you do not have to concern yourself about what he will do. If you make a man feel that he is inferior, you do not have to compel him to accept an inferior status, for he will seek it himself. If you make a man think that he is justly an outcast, you do not have to order him to the back door. He will go without being told; and if there is no back door, his very nature will demand one."*

*- Carter G. Woodson*

Dr. Carter G. Woodson's words, quoted above, were written almost 100 years ago, but they continue to provide the clearest and most succinct account of the Belief Gap that continues to persist in the minds of African-Americans in general and African-American children in particular. In fact, for anyone who has a sincere desire to understand the Belief Gap, Dr. Woodson's book, *Mis-education of the Negro*, is required reading.[109]

Harvest Prep, Best Academy, Mastery School, and Sister Academy provide a blueprint for what is possible in closing the Belief Gap. This section starts off with an excerpt from Claudia Payne's Harvest Prep 8th grade graduation speech. It offers a painful account, from a child's perspective, of the low expectations that many African-American students face in schools around the country.

*Hello my name is Claudia Payne. "If you can Dream it, you can do it!" This quote is by Walt Disney! It means that if you have a goal or a vision for something, you are going to get it done. It will take a lot of hard work and dedication in order to achieve the goal or vision. If you do, then it shall and will be done.*

*Although this was my first year at Harvest I have had many positive experiences. One positive experience from this year that I will always remember is my classmates, for always pushing me to be myself and to never give up on myself. I came from a school known as Robert E. Lee Middle School, where African American kids were not known as high achievers. We were looked down on, as, "Oh those kids they will never get anywhere in life." But when I came to Harvest I felt I can be somebody in life and that I have a future..."*

It's pretty certain that no one at Robert E. Lee School said to Claudia or the other African-American students at that school that the school had low expectations for the Black students. But in far too many subtle, and even not so subtle ways, the message was very clear: "We don't expect much from African-American students." This message is communicated in both urban and even suburban schools that have plenty of resources and are strongly supported by parents. Later in this section, the phenomenon known as the Pygmalion Effect will help to explain how these negative messages of low expectations are communicated by teachers and other adults in the school to poor children and children of color. Despite greater resources in suburban schools, there remains a substantial achievement gap between African American students and White students.

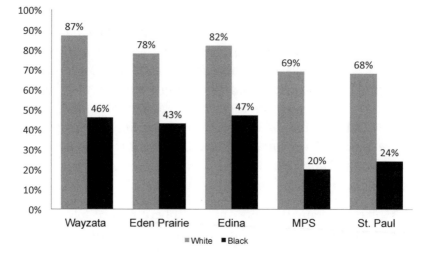

Figure 32. Minnesota's Math Achievement Gap; Urban and Suburban School Districts, 2012.

As Figure 32 illustrates the achievement gap is not simply a city or urban phenomenon. As referred to in the introduction of the book, the achievement gap is just as prevalent in Minnesota's most affluent suburban school districts (Wayzata, Eden Prairie, and Edina) as it is in the urban school districts. The average home in Wayzata is valued at $400,000, while the average home in Minneapolis is valued at $134,000. African-American families that live in these affluent suburbs are paying almost $300,000 more for their homes, due in large part, to the promise of a better education. But while their children may be doing slightly better than African-American children in the city, the Black/White achievement gap is almost as wide as it is in city schools. What accounts for the 75–90% achievement gap in these most affluent suburban school districts? It's directly related to the Belief Gap.

## Effective Effort versus Innate Ability

Americans in general suffer from a pervasive belief that people are born with a certain amount of intelligence, and no matter what people do, they cannot affect their innate intellectual ability.

Dr. Harold Stevenson, in his book *The Learning Gap*,[110] provides compelling evidence that the best American schools are worse than the worst Asian schools. The difference in performance, he writes, has nothing to do with genetics and everything to do with culture. He demonstrates this fundamental difference between Asian and American culture in a survey that was given to a group of students from Asia and a group of students from America. Dr. Stevenson asked the American students the following question: If they had to choose between two ingredients, hard work and innate ability, which one would be the most important ingredient for success. The American students consistently answered that innate ability was the most important ingredient for success. When Dr. Stevenson asked the Asian students the same question, their response was that hard work was the most important ingredient for success. In American culture either you have it (innate ability) or you don't. In Asian culture if you don't have it, all you have to do is work hard for it and you will get it (effective effort).

In education this constitutes a significant and powerful difference in mindset. This mindset that innate ability is the most important ingredient for success has been extremely debilitating for American children in general. It has been particularly debilitating for African-American children; that's because of the historical stereotype of the intellectual inferiority that has been cast upon African-Americans, a stereotype that has been used over the centuries to justify various forms of disparate treatment and institutional racism that originated with slavery.

Thomas Jefferson, the second president of the United States and the principal author of one of the most profound institutional documents, the Declaration of Independence, begins its preamble with the acknowledgment that "we hold these truths to be self-evident, that all men are created equal." Yet in 1781 Jefferson wrote "I advance it, therefore, as a suspicion only, that the blacks, whether originally a distinct race, or made distinct by time and circumstances, are inferior to the whites in the endowments both of body and mind."[111] Jefferson wrote these words despite the fact that, based on DNA testing, he fathered children with his enslaved African-American mistress, Sally Hemmings. Consider, then, how ingrained this "belief" system of racial inferiority must be; and for those who are quick to say, "Oh, that was more than 300 years ago," consider the following:

In the late 1960s Arthur Jensen published a report in the *Harvard Educational Review*—a publication that automatically gave it credibility, which concluded that programs like Head Start failed because about 70% of IQ was fixed at birth (i.e., innate ability). And as late as 1994, two Harvard professors, Richard Hernstein and Charles Murray, wrote a racially provocative book, which continued to promote the idea of racial inferiority based on pseudo-science, called *The Bell Curve. The Bell Curve* was a 600-page diatribe justifying the theory of innate ability. It became controversial because it espoused the belief that innate intelligence was not evenly distributed amongst the races, and argued that Blacks were not as intelligent as Whites, and that this lack of intelligence predicted both economic and social disparities amongst the races.

The effect of drinking the innate-ability Kool-Aid has taken its toll on American children in general, and White and African-American children in particular. In general it has affected American children, because of the xenophobic belief that Americans are superior to all people of the world; it has affected White children in particular because of the belief that they are superior to all other races; and it has affected African-American children in particular because the idea of racial inferiority permeates all of our institutions and systems.

This belief of racial inferiority was made self-evident by Dr. Kenneth Clark in studies that were used as evidence in the case of *Brown v. Board of Education*—the U.S. Supreme Court decision that struck down the legal principle of "separate but equal". Between 1939 and 1940, Dr. Kenneth Clark and his wife Mamie Clark developed what has become popularly known as the *Doll Study*, which was designed to examine the effects of racism and racial segregation on the psyche of Black children. A team of psychologists led by Dr. and Mrs. Clark conducted an experiment showing Black dolls and White dolls to African-American children who attended racially segregated schools in the south and integrated schools in the north. When African-American children were asked which doll was pretty, most of them chose the White doll. When asked which doll was the nicest doll, most of them chose the White doll. The experiment exposed the deeply internalized effects of racism, which showed a clear preference for the White doll among all children in the study, but which was more acute among children attending segregated schools. Dr. Clark believed that the primary cause of this self-rejection and denial was based on segregation. However, subsequent reenactments of the *Doll Study* suggest that the feelings of racial inferiority still felt by African-American children, even today, may have very little to do with racial segregation.

The Kenneth and Mamie Clark *Doll Study* has been reenacted for the past 70 years with similar results, even decades after American society experienced integration. This suggests that the mindset of inferiority clearly has to do with more than just segregation. In 2005, Kiri Davis, a young African-American filmmaker, conducted a new *Doll Study* similar to that of Dr. and Mrs. Clark.[112] Once again, when Davis asked the children which child looks good, the majority of African-American children picked the White doll. When Davis asked the children which doll looked bad, the majority of the children picked the Black doll. Probably the most disturbing part of the experiment came with the follow-up question. After one of the young African-American girls chose the Black doll as being the bad doll, she was asked which doll resembled her. After struggling with the internal conflict, the girl pushed the Black doll forward to Davis.

Returning to the question of the achievement gap, the question we must ask ourselves is this: How can children have any confidence in their intelligence when they look in the mirror every day and see something that looks "bad" and "dumb"?

As recently as 2009, CNN journalist Anderson Cooper did his own doll study on CNN and asked similar questions of both African-American and White children. He presented a poster board that had six pictures of a girl. The pictures were exactly the same with the exception of the color of the girl's skin and hair. Cooper asked the children these questions: "Which picture looks nice? Which picture would you like to be your friend? Which picture do you think most adults like?" Then, going directly to the issue of intelligence, he asked: "Which child is dumb and which child is smart?" As was the case over 70 years ago when Dr. Kenneth Clark conducted his study, the majority of African-American children and the majority of White children identified the images of African-American children as having all the negative attributes. But the problem goes beyond children. Adults hold the same attitudes and beliefs. *The Implicit Association Test*—developed by social psychologists at the University of Washington and Harvard University—confirms that most Americans share the same attitudes of racial bias as demonstrated by the children in the doll studies.[113]

## The Crooked Room

In one study experimenters created a "crooked room." That is, they made everything in the room crooked. The chairs were crooked, the tables were crooked, and even the pictures on the walls were crooked. The subjects were placed in a crooked chair in a crooked room and then asked to align themselves vertically. Some perceived themselves as straight only in relation to their surroundings. To researchers' surprise some people could be tilted as much as 35 degrees and report that they were perfectly straight, simply because they were aligned with images that were equally tilted. But not everyone did this: some managed to get themselves more or less upright regardless of how crooked the surrounding images were.

*When they confront race and gender stereotypes, black women are standing in a crooked room, and they have to figure out which way is up. Bombarded with warped images of their humanity, some black women tilt and bend themselves to fit the distortion.*[114]

Dr. Melissa V. Harris-Perry uses the Crooked Room study as a metaphor to highlight Black women's struggle to find "their upright" position in a room that is projecting a distorted reflection of them. This same metaphor also applies to the distorted messages and images projected onto all Black people, men and women alike, about their intellectual ability. Noted educator and anti-racism activist Jane Elliott has conducted similar classroom experiments, such as the powerful Blue Eyes/Brown Eyes experiment, in which students with blue eyes are singled out for disparate treatment and ridiculed because of the color of their eyes. The experiment highlights the similarity of the treatment of blue-eyed students to that of Black people and Native Americans. This psychological warfare has been going on for hundreds of years, and it continues today, manifesting in such things as cartoon portrayals of President Barack Obama as a monkey with big ears. Many Black people find it impossible to find their upright position, because they don't even realize that they are in a crooked room, in which the reflection of them is distorted. They learn to see these crooked images as being normal or straight, and adjust themselves in a similarly crooked manner.

Unjust laws, like Jim Crow, voting rights, cultural norms, and even medical diagnoses were developed specifically for African-American people to distort the image of their humanity. These laws and cultural norms made the crazy seem normal and the normal seem crazy. Slave codes, Black codes, separate and unequal treatment under the "law," and other crooked laws were used to distort the rights of African-American people and communicate to them and others that they were less than human. Pseudo-science was even created to give pseudo-psychological and medical diagnoses to African-American people's natural desire to be free. In 1851 a physician by the name of Dr. Samuel A. Cartwell developed a diagnosis that was applied to any slave who wanted to, or actually did, run away from his master. This psychological condition was called *Drapetomania* - the runaway slave disease.

### Stereotype Threat

This belief of racial inferiority is taken a step further by Dr. Claude Steele in his work on *Stereotype Threat*. Stereotype threats are stereotypes and beliefs that impact our performance in life, in general, and academic achievement, in particular. Stereotype threats exist when a person's actions confirm the stereotype of one's particular ethnic group.

Dr. Steele demonstrates the existence of stereotype threats in experiments he conducted on students at Stanford University, a school that requires high academic performance for admission. Yet Dr. Steele continued to find the same latent beliefs of inferiority among high-performing African-American students. The experiment took high-performing African-American students with superior high school grades and high SAT scores and matched them with high-performing White students. He then gave both groups a rigorous academic test and told them that the test was a test of their ability—*ability* being the code word that turns on the stereotype. Most of the African- American students did significantly poorer on the test than the White students. Dr. Steele then repeated the test with a second group of African-American students whose academic credentials were similar to those of the first set of African-Americans. However, Steele said nothing to them about the test being a test of ability. In this second test, the African-American students did as well as the White students.

What these tests tell us is that we live in a culture that feeds African-American children a hardy and unhealthy dose of self-rejection, denial, self-doubt, and intellectual inferiority—a dose that manifests itself today in the achievement gap. The question is whether this negative image that many of us have of African-Americans, and that African-American children have of themselves, can be healed. Can the mindset of children be changed from believing in innate ability to believing in the importance of effective effort? In other words can children come to believe, as Dr. Jeff Howard espouses, that "Smart is not who you are; but, rather, smart is what you become through hard work"?[115]

### The Great Debate (Structural, Cultural, or Beliefs)

There is a current debate in academia as to whether the poor academic performance of low-income children of color is a structural problem or a cultural problem.[116] As Professor Pedro Noguera[117] states in his book, *The Trouble with Black Boys*, structuralists generally believe that the political economy is the source of the problem—the availability of jobs and economic opportunities, class structure, and social geography. From this perspective individuals are viewed as products of their environment, and changes in individual behavior are made possible by changes in the structure of opportunity. The structuralist believes that holding an individual responsible for his or her behavior makes little sense since behavior is shaped by the forces beyond the control of any particular individual. Drug abuse, crime, and dropping out of school are largely seen as social consequences of inequality. According to this view the most effective way to reduce objectionable behavior is to reduce the degree and the extent of inequality in society. Staunch advocates of integration would be considered structuralists. The structuralist worldview tells part of the story. There are, indeed, structural inequalities that pose barriers to academic achievement for economically and socially disadvantaged children, as was discussed in Chapter 2 on social costs.

In contrast, culturalists downplay the significance of environmental factors on human behavior. Culturalists see human behavior as a product of beliefs, values, norms, and socialization. Cultural explanations of behavior focus on the moral code that operates within the particular family, communities, or groups.

For example, the idea that poor people are trapped within a "culture of poverty," which has the effect of legitimizing criminal and immoral behavior, has dominated the culturalist perspective of poverty. For the culturalist changes in behavior can be brought about only through cultural change. Hence, providing more money to inner-city schools or busing inner-city children to affluent suburban schools will do little to improve their academic performance since their attitudes towards school are shaped by the culture brought from home and the neighborhood. According to this view, culture provides the rationale and the motivation for behavior, and cultural change cannot be brought about through changes in government policy or by expanding opportunities.

**The Involuntary Minority**

Contributing to the belief gap is perhaps a more pernicious belief gap among African-Americans themselves. This belief gap involves African-Americans' distrust of the dominant culture and its institutions, including its schools.[118] Another example of the culturalists view expressed by Dr. Noguera is that of educational anthropologist, John Ogbu. Ogbu has offered a theory based on a voluntary versus involuntary minority typology.[119]

Under Ogbu's hypothesis voluntary minorities—those who chose to immigrate to a host country—view the host society's institutions, including schools, as an opportunity. For example, Africans, West Indians, and Asians who have immigrated from their home countries to the United States, view the schools in terms of what they can gain from them. Likewise, they view teachers as experts in specific areas and as the source of the knowledge they need. Even if they face discrimination, they do not internalize the mistreatment. Rather, they remain focused on the opportunity to gain valuable knowledge and skills. They are also willing to learn, accept, and adapt to the cultural norms of the majority group. They see no threat to their own identity as a result of adopting new behaviors. In fact, they expect to learn new ways as necessary for success in the host country.

According to Ogbu voluntary minorities are steady academic achievers.[120] There are many examples of this in Minnesota, which has become home to large communities of Asian and East African refugees from such countries as Cambodia, Laos, and Somalia. In fact, Minnesota has the largest Hmong and Somali communities in the entire United States. The first generations of students from these communities were high achievers; Hmong and Somali students were found at the top honor of their classes.[121]

Involuntary minorities—those who did not choose their minority status through emigration, but rather occupy that demographic status as a result of conquest, forced migration, or enslavement (e.g., African-Americans and Native Americans)—have an oppositional approach to schools. In fact, in psychological terms, they might be classified as oppositional defiant. Because of long periods of discrimination by the dominant culture and its institutions, involuntary minorities have developed responses and behaviors that emphasize their distrust of, and opposition to, the dominant society and its institutions. In addition, they sustain alternative, self-affirming norms and values that maintain boundaries between them and the majority—norms and values that often undermine academics.[122] Further, the actions and attitudes of involuntary minorities reflect the fact that they come to school with distinctive cultural and language patterns that distinguish them from the majority cultural behaviors, for example, sagging pants, sexually explicit clothing, sideways caps, cursing, talking slang, and not wanting to "sound or act White." In fact, they will even defend their "alternative" behaviors, even though they facilitate academic failure. Some involuntary minority parents will defend their children and attack teachers and administrators even when their children have engaged in such aberrant behavior as hitting or cursing a teacher. Rather than adapting their behaviors for maximum efficiency and efficacy in the quest for academic success, involuntary minorities according to Ogbu "will devote disproportionate effort fighting for political, social, and economic equality with the dominant group members."[123]

Any casual observer of our educational system will find ample evidence of Ogbo's theory. Recent findings from the Minneapolis Foundation report, *One Minneapolis*, offer glimpses of support for the voluntary versus involuntary minority theory: The employment gap between Whites and Native Americans is 27 percentage points, and between Whites and U.S.-born Blacks is 25 percentage points. But the employment gap between foreign-born Blacks and White is just 10 percentage points. In the area of education, Hispanic and African (not African-American) students in Minneapolis Public Schools are most likely to report that their teachers make them want to learn, than are African-American and Native-American students.

In order to reform the system, we must understand the beliefs of those we seek to change. Teachers and school leaders, and indeed all of us involved in the education of children, must understand how we arrived at our current condition in order to effect a change. We must reduce the pervasive distrust between school boards and administrators, administrators and teachers, teachers and parents, and teachers and students.

We must also change the media bias about what can be achieved. In the *StarTribune* little attention is given to the achievement of the Minneapolis Public Schools in general, and African-American students in particular. Instead, the constant drumbeat is its failures. In 2011, when Harvest Prep and Best Academy students busted the myth of the achievement gap by outscoring the statewide average in both reading and math, the headline in the *StarTribune* read, "Math Scores Disappointing". Buried in the middle of the three-page article was a two-sentence mention of the fact that, despite a statewide decline in math scores, Best Academy 8th grade students were 85% proficient. In reading, Best Academy boys scored a perfect 100% proficient, but little was made of this outstanding achievement. In order for the belief gap to change, the media representation must change.

We have to deal with people's beliefs about each other and have conversations about the underlying beliefs. We need to recognize and understand that public beliefs and values are not always congruent. In order to close the achievement gap, positive information on African-American and Native American students and the African-American and Native American community must be provided. Materials must be created that stress positive school models that provide excellence and equity in schools serving high numbers of African-American and Native-American students, like Harvest Prep, Best Academy, Friendship Academy, Hiawatha Academy in Minneapolis, and Higher Ground Academy in St. Paul.

## Creating a New Mindset

*Schools that do not have an effective strategy for convincing students to become invested in their education – to work hard, study, arrive at school on time and prepared, and generally care about learning, are unlikely to reduce disparities in academic outcomes and raise student achievement.*

*– Pedro Noguera*

Dr. Carol Dweck, a Stanford University social and developmental psychologist, has written two books on creating a new mindset. In her first book, *Self-Theories*,[124] she demonstrates that even students who have been identified with a fixed mindset (i.e. a belief in innate ability) can be influenced to believe in a growth mindset (i.e. effective effort). In one of Dr. Dweck's experiments, a group of psychologists used articles to influence college students' theories of intelligence. They asked entering freshmen about their interest in remedial English courses that could improve their scholastic performance. The aim of the study was to see if students who had a fixed mindset would pass up the chance to enhance their skill deficits. Half of the students read articles that offered a vivid and convincing version of the fixed mindset (innate ability) theory and the other half read articles that offered a vivid and convincing version of the growth mindset (effective effort) theory.

After answering questions about what they read, the students took a nonverbal ability test. The students were then grouped into two categories, based on their test results—those who had done relatively well and those who had done relatively poorly. The two groups of students were then offered a tutorial that had been proven effective for most people at improving performance on the test.

The study found that most of the students who had performed well on the test wanted to take the tutorial, regardless of whether they were in the fixed (innate ability) mindset group, or the growth (effective effort) mindset. However, among those who had done poorly, the story was starkly different. Most of the students (73.3%) who were exposed to the growth (effective effort) mindset theory still wanted to take the tutorial to improve their performance; but very few (13.3%) of the students who had been exposed to the fixed (innate ability) mindset wanted to take the tutorial to improve their skills. The study concluded that when students have a fixed (innate ability) view of intelligence, those that need the most help and remediation are the ones who most clearly avoid it.

For low-income African-American and other ethnic students, a fixed mindset is detrimental to the goal of academic achievement and continuous improvement. Many students come to Harvest Prep and Best Academy two and three grade levels behind. Not only does the school have to provide an effective curriculum, time and human resources to get students caught up academically, but its teachers and administrators must also understand that many students are behind and stay behind because they have been brainwashed into believing that they cannot achieve. Either consciously or subconsciously, these students believe that they were born with a certain amount of intelligence and that additional academic support and effort on their part would be a waste of time.

In another experiment Dweck showed that students' mindsets could be changed from a fixed (innate ability) mindset to a growth (effective effort) mindset. Dweck gave African-American college students a psychological assessment to determine with what kind of mindset the students were operating. Those with a fixed mindset were given specific training on the power of the growth mindset and how the brain develops. They were then asked to teach this new theory of intelligence (growth mindset) to elementary students. Several months later the African-American students were surveyed again, and they demonstrated a significant change in their beliefs. Improved grades also reflected the positive change in mindset.

As educators and as a society, we must first believe that the brain is like a muscle, and then we must use every method possible to convince these students that this is true. Just as a bicep in the arm will grow from continuous exercise, a student will make academic progress from continuous mental exercise.

One way to convince students about the growth mindset is to give them examples of people who have improved themselves academically—and in their careers—through effective effort. It is possible to change a child's belief system by giving her or him examples of how others have overcome significant obstacles by applying the growth mindset, and by celebrating and rewarding students who demonstrate effective effort on a regular basis. At Harvest Prep and Best Academy considerable and explicit effort is expended to make it plain that teachers, administrators, and all of the adults in the student's life, highly value effective effort.

### Teacher Beliefs/Expectations

Research shows that teachers' expectations strongly influence students' effort and performance.[125] High expectations for student achievement (pressure to learn) have been one of the most consistent findings in the literature. Virtually every review of the topic—whether British, Dutch, or American—mentions the importance of this factor.[126] High expectations rank second among school-level factors that impact student achievement.[127]

### The Pygmalion Effect [128]

In 1968 Robert Rosenthal and Lenore Jacobson conducted a school-wide experiment that has become known as the Pygmalion Effect. The name Pygmalion was taken from a play by George Bernard Shaw, which posited the notion that the greater the expectations placed upon people, the better they perform.

Rosenthal and Jacobson told the teachers that some students in their classroom were considered "late intellectual bloomers," based upon a pseudo- psychological test that the experimenters had created and administered. Rosenthal and Jacobson did not tell the students that they were late bloomers—only the teachers. They told the teachers that these students were expected to bloom by the end of the school year.

What Rosenthal and Jacobson wanted to show was how a teacher's positive expectations can impact a student's intellectual ability. Rosenthal tested every elementary student in the school with the test that they said would predict academic blooming. The made-up test was called the Harvard Test of Inflected Acquisition. In reality, the children selected as late bloomers were selected at random. The children didn't know, in any direct way, that the teachers' expectations of them were any different.

When they tested the students a year later, those students that had been identified as the intellectual late bloomers showed significantly higher academic gains than the ones who had not been so identified. In other words the children got smarter when they were expected to get smarter by their teachers.

The researchers found four factors that operated in the communication of the teachers' self-fulfilling prophecies. The first factor they identified was the *climate factor*. Teachers tended to create a warmer climate for students for whom they had higher expectations. They tended to be nicer to the students, both in the things they said and in their nonverbal communication. The second factor was the *input factor*. Teachers taught more rigorous material to those students for whom they had higher expectations. The teachers did not teach the same high level of material to students for whom they did not have high expectations. The third factor was the response to the *opportunity factor*. Students got many chances to respond when teachers had high expectations of them. Teachers called on these students more often.

When they called on these students, they also let them talk longer. Teachers also tended to work longer with those students for whom they had higher expectations, even to the point of developing answers to the questions they had asked if the students were having trouble answering them. The last factor observed was *feedback*. The higher the teacher's expectation of the student, the more praise the student received. Students received more positive reinforcement not only for giving a good answer, but also even when they gave the wrong answer; and students for whom they had higher expectations, the teacher was observed guiding them towards the right answer. The consistent and persistent achievement gap between Black children and White children, in both urban and suburban school districts, is a direct result of (a) what Black students have learned to believe about their innate capabilities and (b) the pervasive Pygmalion Effect that teachers unconsciously harbor about the innate ability of African- American children. If anyone doubts that the Pygmalion Effect still exists, please reread Claudia Payne's account of her experience in her suburban school and then re-review Figure 32 that compares urban and suburban school performance.

As further evidence the 2010 *One Minneapolis* report found that Native American and Black children (which includes African and African-American) were least likely to report that their teachers motivated them to learn. Almost one-third of Black students in Minneapolis Public Schools reported that they were not motivated to learn because of their teachers' style of teaching. The report concluded that this fact may point to instructional methods that are less effective among these students, a less nurturing relationship between these students and their teachers, or both.

### Debunking the Myth That Poverty and Ethnicity Result in Low Achievement

From 1995 to 2000, the Center for Performance Assessment (an educational consulting firm based in Denver, Colorado) conducted a five-year assessment of students in a variety of school settings, from elementary through high school. The study was called *90/90/90 Schools: A Case Study.*[129]

The study is significant because its findings debunk the hypothesis—still prevalent among many educators today—that poverty and ethnicity are inextricably linked to lower levels of student achievement. This hypothesis, dating back to the 1960s, leaves no room for schools that have high academic achievement that is coincident with high poverty and high minority enrollment. The study concluded that while the impact of poverty has not been eliminated, the prevailing hypothesis—that poor minority students are destined to perform poorly—does not conform to the data.

One of the significant findings from the 2010 Minneapolis Public Schools *Kindergarten Readiness Study* as it relates to the Belief Gap was that the primary home language, race, and ethnicity were not statistically significant predictors of kindergarten readiness. Income, however, was a statistically significant predictor. The same finding was made in the early childhood study, conducted in 1998 by the University of Michigan for the U.S. Department of Education, entitled *Inequality at the Starting Gate*, involving 16,000 kindergarten children. Both studies found that income, more than race, correlated with cognitive skills. They debunk the myth (i.e. belief) that a child's academic ability has anything to do with his or her race or ethnicity. It's a shame that this conversation persists into the 21st century.

## There are Lower Expectations for, and More Frequent Punishment of, African-American Students

Stacks of research reports indicate that attitudes towards, and expectations of, African-American students are lower and more negative than for White students. In fact, many African-American parents and students have lower expectations of performance, particularly the older the students become. African American students are not given the same opportunities to participate in enriched educational offerings, and they are more frequently removed from the general education classroom due to misclassification by special education policies and practices.[130]

At present, large racial disparities mark the participation rates in more rigorous or advanced courses, and in high school, advanced placement (AP) coursework. Nationally, White male students are more than twice as likely as Black male students to be placed in gifted/talented programs and four times more likely to take AP math and science classes. Conversely, Black male students are more than twice as likely as White male students to be classified as mentally retarded—despite research demonstrating that the percentage of students from all groups is approximately the same at each intelligence level.[131]

According to the National Education Policy Center (NEPC) at the University of Colorado, in 2006-2007 (the latest year for which data were available) African-American students were suspended nationally three times as often as White students (15% vs. 5%). In addition, minorities and disabled children are more often suspended for minor offenses. In Minneapolis the rate of suspension for African-American students compared to White students is twice the national average. During the 2009-2010 school year, Black students were six times more likely to be suspended than White students.[132] In fact, three-fourths of all students suspended from Minneapolis Public Schools were African-American. According to the 2011 *One Minneapolis* report, one in four African-American boys is suspended once or more per year.[133] And, of the African-American students who are suspended, the average is three suspensions a year. Consistent with these findings, the *One Minneapolis* report found that African-American boys are least likely to trust adults in school to keep them safe, and African-American residents are most likely to feel unaccepted because of their race, ethnicity, or culture.

### The Bannister Effect

Eric Mahmoud has developed a theory about the achievement gap that he calls the Bannister Effect, which takes its name from 1950s long-distance runner, Roger Bannister. He was the first person ever to run the mile in under four minutes. Until Bannister accomplished the feat, no one believed that it was humanly possible to run a mile in less than four minutes. But after Bannister, many other runners continually and consistently broke the presumed four-minute barrier. Mahmoud theorizes that once someone demonstrates that the achievement gap can be closed for African-American students, many will believe that it can be done. Now that Harvest Prep and Best Academy have provided a model of high achievement, Mahmoud expects many other schools to follow.

### There Must Be a No-Excuses Expectation That All Children Can Achieve

It goes without saying that every student has a different achievement level and that some students will outperform others. But among school leaders and teachers there must be an uncompromising belief that all children can achieve proficiency in core subjects like math, reading, and science regardless of race, ethnicity, income, or circumstances. Research has shown—not that proof was needed—that all children, regardless of race, or ethnicity, are endowed with the same intellectual capabilities. Take Hakim, for example. He came to live with his aunt and uncle in the 5th grade. When he arrived he was two or three grade levels behind in reading and math. Nevertheless, by the end of his 5th grade year, he was reading at grade level, and by the end of his 6th grade year, he was one of Harvest's top academic performers, exceeding statewide standards in both reading and math. This was the same Hakim. Nothing had changed about the hardware (i.e. the mind) of Hakim, but there was now a belief and a no-excuses commitment that, given the academic support he needed, Hakim could, and indeed would, achieve.

It is our responsibility to first believe and then to ensure that all students achieve academic success. We can no longer make excuses for why African-American and low-income children are not excelling in the classroom. Anyone with wisdom and insight who has taught African-American children knows that the nascent abilities of African-American children are equal to any other children. It is the responsibility of school leaders and teachers to reignite this innate desire in children to learn, to reignite the fire where it has grown dim, and to add fuel where it continues to shine bright.

### Laser-Like Focus on Student Achievement

In the *90/90/90 Study* referred to earlier, profound differences were discovered in the "beliefs" of 90/90/90 schools and low-achieving schools. First and foremost the 90/90/90 schools had a laser-like focus on student achievement. Charts, graphs, and tables on student achievement, including continuous improvement, filled the hallways. Trophy cases contained not just trophies of athletic achievement, but exemplary academic work.

It goes without saying that this is particularly important in an environment where many students come to school with academic skills that are substantially below grade level. They must be given this message consistently: It's not how you start, but how you finish.

### All Students Must be Offered More Rigorous Curriculum Choices

To even out the educational disparities, students of all races—not just some—need to be offered a challenging, but realistic curriculum beginning in elementary school so they are prepared to take more rigorous or advanced courses in secondary school.[134] If everyone is taught challenging content, everyone is much more likely to learn challenging content. The focus must be on academic achievement.[136] There should be clear curriculum choices that allow and direct students to take more challenging content. As practiced in countries that are outperforming the U.S., the curriculum should identify essential learning and emphasize depth over breadth and quality over quantity.[137]

# 6

## How We Get It Done

*People who say it can't be done should not interrupt those who are doing it.*

—*George Bernard Shaw*

**Case Study 6: Amina**

Amina attended Harvest Prep from preschool through the 5th grade. Her mother was the most resourceful parent that Eric Mahmoud had ever known. Even though she had been receiving government assistance for most of Amina's childhood, this didn't stop her from enrolling Amina in every academic and talent enrichment program available since kindergarten.

As an elementary school student, Amina attended the Imhotep Science Academy when she was five years old. The Academy is named after the Egyptian architect, doctor, priest, poet, and astrologist, Imhotep, who is credited with designing and building the first pyramid in Egypt. The mission of the Academy is to inspire African-American youth to use their scientific thinking to solve problems in the African-American community. Amina participated in Microsoft's DigiGirlz Camp, which exposes girls to technology in order to motivate them to consider careers in technology. Amina was also a student ambassador for the People to People international travel program, which takes students on cultural and historic explorations around the world to develop their cultural awareness and global perspective. Amina spent part of a summer in England.

As a middle school student, Amina founded a girl's organization called Girls in Motion that helped to shape the cultural and political thinking of girls and adults around the Twin Cities. The organization sponsored youth seminars, as well as college tours. For the impact she made through her organization, Amina was awarded the prestigious Dare to Dream grant in 2010 from the Ann Bancroft Foundation. Named after one of the world's preeminent polar explorers and an internationally recognized leader, the foundation awards the grant to inspire girls and women around the world to unleash the power of their dreams.

At the age of 16, Amina spent a year in China studying Chinese language and culture. Upon return she participated in the Breakthrough Collaborative, a program designed to give middle and high school students the opportunity to teach during the summer.

Colleges recruited Amina like they recruit All-American high school athletes. She finally chose Hillary Clinton's alma mater, Wellesley College in Massachusetts. Along with her rigorous course load, she leads many student organizations.

The overview of Amina's extracurricular experiences is only a brief summary of all that she has accomplished. A book could be written just on Amina and her incredible life journey. Amina is one of many examples of what's possible for African-American children if they have adults in their lives that believe in their intellectual capacity, and if they are willing to research, work hard, and be persistent.

The Gap-Closing Framework that follows is the model developed and honed at Harvest Prep and Best Academy. As the reader will see, it is not new. It is based on the successful practice of schools from around the country that have excelled in teaching students who would be considered educationally disadvantaged by reason of income, wealth, ethnicity, and geographic location.

### The Gap-Closing Framework

Harvest Prep and Best Academy use an educational model patterned after high-performing public schools. It is built around the five essential questions that have been repeatedly mentioned, taken from Richard Dufour's book *Learning by Doing*. Schools that have answered these five essential questions have demonstrated success serving children from low-income backgrounds.

1. What do my students need to know and be able to do?
2. What are the most effective ways to teach what they need to know?
3. How do I know that they got it?
4. If they didn't get it after I taught it, then what?
5. What if they have already mastered the material before I taught it?

### The Gap-Closing Framework

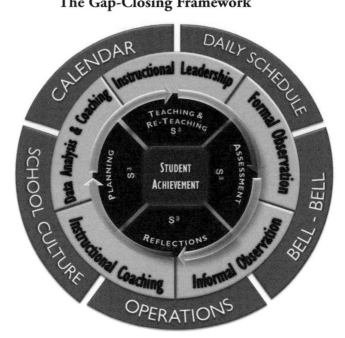

Figure 33. The Gap-Closing Framework, 2011.

To answer these five questions, Harvest Prep and Best Academy use the Gap-Closing Framework in Figure 33. It is designed from the inside out and organized around a set of concentric rings. Because student achievement is the *sine qua non* of teaching, student achievement is found at the center of the ring. Because the greatest lever that influences student achievement is teaching, the teaching ring is placed in symbiotic relationship with the core of the framework with student achievement.

The teaching ring is composed of (a) Planning, (b) Teaching and Re-teaching, (c) Assessment, (d) Reflection and Student Support Systems (abbreviated as S3). Everything in the middle and outer rings supports teaching and learning. The middle ring of administration supports teaching. The administrative ring is composed of Instructional Leadership, Formal and Informal Observations, Instructional Coaching, and Data Analysis and Coaching. The outer ring, which supports teaching and administration, consists of the academic and operational supports that ensure the most effective teaching and administration. It is composed of School Culture, Operations, Bell to Bell (class time), the Daily Schedule, and the (yearly) Calendar.

Note that the Instructional Leadership model supports teaching, but it does not drive the teaching model; similarly, the Calendar supports the teaching model, but it does not drive it.

As discussed in Chapter 5, the standard public school year of 180 days, with a 6.5-hour school day, provides insufficient learning time to cover all of the benchmarks and standards that students are expected to learn. Consequently, at Harvest Prep and Best Academy both the school year and school day have been expanded. This ensures sufficient learning time, thus maximizes student achievement. It reflects an emphasis on the fundamental question: what do students need to maximize achievement? Harvest Prep and Best Academy worked backwards to make sure that all of the supports, systems, and structures were in place to meet those needs.

By expanding the school year, another obstacle for low-income students was removed: the summertime learning gap. A three-month vacation is appreciated by teachers, but it jeopardizes the progress of students, particularly those who are further behind and in the greatest need. No other profession commands the four months of vacation afforded to teachers (three months of summer vacation, two weeks of winter/Christmas break, one week of spring/Easter break, and a week of other holidays interspersed throughout the year). While there has been union resistance to reducing the summer vacation for teachers, a compromise has been achieved by some high-performing schools: extend the school year, while interspersing vacation time more evenly throughout the year at 1–2-week intervals. This has proven effective in increasing student achievement and avoiding the summertime learning gap.

In many public school districts and schools, however, the educational framework operates in just the opposite manner. Administration starts with the school calendar, daily schedule, and operations, and then tries to figure out how to fit everything into those fixed structures. Instead of changing the size of the educational box by adding more learning time, administrators and teachers are forced to work within a time structure that has proven inadequate and ineffective. Hearkening back to the words of former Minneapolis Public Schools Superintendent, Dr. Carol Johnson, "In our public education system, time is justice. What is enough time for some is not enough time for others."

In sum, these structures do not help solve the educational challenges that economically disadvantaged and minority children face—children who start kindergarten behind and fall further behind through the years. These children need more time to get caught up, not less time.

Schools and school districts that have proven effective in closing the achievement gap design the structure around the vision, mission, and goals in order to optimize student achievement. To reiterate: Student achievement comes first, and everything else revolves around that. Student achievement is at the core of the gap closing framework.

### Inner Ring 1: The Teaching Cycle

The first ring around student achievement is the Teaching Ring. The cycle within this ring proceeds in the following order: Planning, Teaching & Re-teaching, Assessments, and Reflection.[139]

*Guides, forms, and samples of documents from the planning, teaching & re-teaching, assessments, and reflection sections can be found at http://ericmahmoud.com.*

### Planning

Planning addresses the first of the five essential questions set forth at the beginning of this chapter: What do my children need to know and be able to do? Planning comes first in the process, before teaching, assessment, reflection and student support systems. Actually, planning also includes each of these items.

State academic standards provide the guidelines for developing curriculum at Harvest Prep and Best Academy. In every subject area, teachers must ensure that all benchmarks in the state standards are met before year's end.

The link from the state standards to instruction is created by backwards planning. It means starting with the standards established by the state department of education for each subject area and then developing curriculum based on each benchmark that the student is expected to master at that grade level. For example, a 3rd grade reading standard might consist of a student being able to understand "Key Ideas and Details" of a short story. One of the benchmarks under this standard is, "Students will be able to ask and answer questions to demonstrate understanding of the text, referring explicitly to the text as basis for the answer." An important distinction in the planning for teachers is that they must also determine the level of rigor required to master the standards that will be assessed.

### The Yearly Pacing Guide

After a grade-level team of teachers has determined all of the benchmarks and standards that students will have to learn for the year, a pacing guide is established. The guide indicates when any given benchmark will be taught during the school year and how many academic days will be spent covering that benchmark. It can change and be updated throughout the year, but a working draft is available before the first day of school begins.

### The Term Pacing Guide

After the yearlong pacing guide is established, the term guide is developed. It is a more detailed and comprehensive version of the yearly pacing guide. Not only does it include when a benchmark will be taught in the course of the school year, but it is also what indicates the resources that will be used to teach the benchmark and how the benchmark will be assessed to ascertain if students have learned the information. The term pacing guide focuses on one term's progress, highlights the standards or benchmarks to be taught during that term, lists the days they will be taught and the daily objectives of the lesson, and addresses any prerequisite skills or knowledge students need to have before they are able to master the benchmark at grade level.

### Weekly Lesson Plans

As the teacher moves forward in the planning process, the planning becomes more detailed. Weekly lesson plans enable instructional leaders to develop their plans more thoroughly to deliver academic content that is rigorous and engaging. Grade-level teams divide up lesson-planning responsibilities based on the individual strengths of the team members. The lesson plan format is Madeline Hunter's framework.[142]

Lesson planning spirals backwards from interim formative assessments, which are created by grade-level teams prior to the beginning of each term. An interim formative assessment is a rigorous test given in class every 6-8 weeks to determine if students have retained the information from past and current benchmarks. In Minnesota, for example, all tested benchmarks for grades 3-8 must be covered by April 1st of each year, when statewide (Minnesota Comprehensive Assessment) testing occurs. For kindergarten through second grade, teachers have the full year to cover grade-level standards. Backwards planning answers the question, what do my students need to know and be able to do?

In planning lessons Harvest Prep and Best Academy extensively use the book *The Skillful Teacher* by Jon Saphier, Mary Ann Haley-Speca, and Robert Gower. The authors outline 21 planning decisions involved in lesson planning that are highly recommended to all teachers and school leaders. We will not go into these 21 planning decisions, except to say that the first 13 are called basic and indispensable decisions, and the last eight are called implementation decisions.

**Teaching and Re-teaching**

Teaching and re-teaching addresses the second of the five essential questions set forth at the beginning of this chapter: What are the most effective ways to teach what they need to know?

It's not uncommon to believe that we are successful in all things that cannot be measured. The same principle applies in teaching. Teachers tend to believe they are more successful in their teaching, when the results are not measured. At Harvest Prep and Best Academy success is evaluated by how successful students are mastering the standards that are being measured.

Thus, the goals of teaching and re-teaching are as follows:

- To cultivate a growth mindset in all students

- To have students master the benchmarks set by the Minnesota Department of Education, as well as the national benchmarks in reading, writing, math, science, and social studies at all grade levels

- To have students make a year or more of academic growth by the end of the school year

- To have all of students (grades 3-8) meet or exceed the standard on the Minnesota Comprehensive Assessments

- To have 100% of students (grades 2-8) make their target growth goals on the Northwest Education Assessment (NWEA)

- To prepare students for college

- To develop students to use good moral judgment and be positive contributors to society and have a desire to give back to their community.

All of these goals are directly measureable. At each step along the way, a quantifiable answer can be given for each and every student. The period is longer, of course, for college bound students; it's also longer for determining whether students are showing good moral judgment and making positive contributions to society, but it is still quantifiable.

Teaching addresses the question, what are the most effective practices to teach whatever students need to know? This question is answered by using the best research on effective instruction available and by giving the teacher extensive professional development. Instructional leaders facilitate ongoing professional development on effective and engaging instructional strategies and by ongoing use of strategic data systems.

### Assessments

Assessments address the third of the five essential questions set forth at the beginning of this chapter: How do I know if they got it?

At the classroom level, there are three timeframes in which to implement re-teaching strategies based upon assessments: daily, weekly, and end-of-term.

### Daily Exit Slips

The teacher can use exit slips (a question or series of short questions to determine whether students understood the subject matter being taught) on a daily basis or at the end of a lesson to determine whether students have mastered the daily objective. This is the quickest way to find out whether an individual student or classroom of students would benefit from some type of re-teaching. A quick analysis of the exit slip can tell the teacher which skill the student is missing. The teacher is given time during their 50-minute preparation period to review exit slips and homework assignments, in order to adjust the next day's lesson. If more than one student has the same problem, the teacher can group the students together and offer a mini-lesson covering the strategy or step that those students missed. If many students had the same problem, the mini-lesson can be taught to the whole group. This skill can also be spiraled into the homework and the *Do Now* for the following day. Do Now is a warm-up exercise that students complete (i.e. "Do now") during the first 5-10 minutes of class, in which they answer a short series of questions about what was taught the previous day. Once again, by planning how classroom time will be used, sufficient time can be set aside to allow for student grouping or differentiation.

### Weekly Quizzes

At the end of each week, the teacher gives a quiz. The quiz is aligned to the benchmarks covered during the week. The daily school schedule gives the teacher time to develop and grade the quizzes. At Harvest Prep and Best Academy, students leave school early every Friday to allow teachers time to analyze quiz and other testing data. After the quiz is given and graded, the teacher fills out a tracker that shows how each student performed on each question. This tracker is a systematic way to determine which skills need to be retaught and to which students. The re-teaching takes place the following week using strategies like mini-lessons to small groups, differentiated independent work, homework, and Do Nows. If 80% of the class does not understand a particular benchmark as evidenced by exit slips, homework, and weekly quizzes, then the benchmark must be retaught to the entire class. On the other hand, if only a few students haven't mastered a particular benchmark, then the benchmark can be retaught during the intervention period mentioned later. Students who master the benchmarks on the weekly quizzes should be offered differentiated work that will push them further.

### Comprehensive Interim Assessments

At the end of the term, which is usually every 6 - 8 weeks, the teacher will administer a Comprehensive Interim Assessment, also known as a COMP. The COMP covers all of the benchmarks taught during the 6–8-week term. Teachers in grades K-8 administer the COMPs and then fill out a tracker that shows student performances during that period. The weekly and COMP trackers let teachers and administrators know whether students are on track for meeting the state standards. The school then provides teachers with a data day at the end of each term to analyze the information and plan a re-teach week. The data day is usually the Friday at the end of the week that students have taken their COMPs. On data days, the students are released from school, but the teachers come to school to analyze data from test results. In order to be more efficient and allow teachers to actually use the data being generated, Harvest Prep and Best Academy use an automated scanner that takes the test information from students' scores and provides a high-level analysis of the data. The scanner automates as many of the teacher functions as possible to create efficiencies. Time that teachers would otherwise use for grading and logging these interim assessments can now be used for analysis of the data.

Teachers then take this data and determine by grade level, class level, and individual student level what kind of consistent patterns are occurring. Did the whole grade level get some question wrong? For example, if there are four 3rd grade classes, data analysis will show which class did the best, which did the worst, and where the discrepancies are occurring.

The most important part of the data day is for teachers to develop re-teaching plans based on the data. The week following the data day is set aside to re-teach skills that were not mastered. Depending on the number of students who did not master the subject matter, re-teaching will be done either in small groups or with the entire class. It is the job of the grade-level team to determine what activities and lessons will be covered to address the needs of all learners.

With independent work, exit slips, and weekly quizzes, a teacher should know which students are proficient on the benchmarks, even before the COMPs are administered. These tests are collectively referred to as continuous formative assessments, and are critical in providing teachers and administrators with up-to-date data for grading and establishing a teaching and re-teaching roadmap for the teacher to follow.

## Response to Intervention/S3

### What if Students Didn't Learn the Material After I Taught It?

Gap-closing schools use a Response to Intervention (RTI) model to provide additional support to students who are behind. In the Gap-Closing Framework illustration, RTI is symbolized by S3 or Student Support System. RTI is the practice of providing high-quality instruction and interventions that match students' needs, and using students' learning rate over time and level of performance to make important educational decisions.

The theory of RTI is that 80% of students should be supported by the curriculum provided to all students. For the 20% of students who may not be successful with the standard curriculum (or *Tier 1* program as it is called), a system of interventions are set up to address students that are right below grade level (i.e. at *Tier 2*) and students that are far below grade level (i.e. at *Tier 3*). A 50-minute intervention block for *Tier 2* and *Tier 3* students is built into the school schedule to address the students' individual needs. For students in elementary school, the intervention may occur during regularly scheduled class time, assuming there are teaching assistants or support in the classroom. For students in middle school, the intervention may be done by a different teaching intervention specialist and in a one-on-one or small group setting.

## Middle Ring 2: Administrative Support to Teachers

### Instructional Leadership

The purpose of Instructional Leadership is to ensure that student learning time is maximized through teacher professional development. Professional development includes four major categories: data and assessment, planning, classroom management, and core instruction presentation. Instructional leadership is supported by building administrators, teacher leaders (coaches) and/or educational consultants.

Every teacher is assigned an instructional leader or coach to help develop and strengthen their instructional effectiveness. Administrators will track student performance results and then assign teachers to administrators, educational consultants, and teacher support based on grade level and subject expertise. Instructional leaders will provide a half hour of feedback based on a 20-30-minute informal observation every other week, or on an as-needed basis. Instructional leaders meet with teachers and complete a Teacher Learning Plan, which is revised every term (i.e. five times throughout the school year). This practice was adopted at Harvest Prep and Best Academy after school leaders attended a training conducted by Dacia Toll, co-founder of Achievement First charter school management organization.

**Formal Observation**

The system for formal observations is derived from Achievement First,[140] Driven by Data, and the System for Teacher and Student Advancement Program (TAP).[141]

Instructional leaders use formal observations to determine staff development needs and to determine additional incentive pay. Teacher performance is evaluated on a scale from 1 to 5: 1 (*poor*), 2 (*below average*), 3 (*proficient*), 4 (*above average*), to 5 (*exemplary*).

Formal observations are conducted three times a year to evaluate a teacher's overall performance. In order to receive incentive pay, a teacher must have a 3.0 average on their formal observation.

The formal observation process consists of the following:

1. A pre-meeting to discuss the teacher's lesson plan
2. An 45 - 60-minute observation
3. A post-observation meeting with the teacher
4. A follow-up in teacher learning plan

**Informal Observation**

Informal observations are used much in the same way a swimming coach improves a swimmer's technique by being at the pool to observe swimming during lessons, practice, and swim meets. *Driven by Data: A Practical Guide to Improve Instruction* by Paul Bambrick-Santoyo[143] has heavily influenced the notion of being "at the pool" to give teachers feedback on their teaching. You can't improve a swimmer's technique by reading about their performance in the newspaper the next day. The coach must be "at the pool" providing feedback to the swimmer minute by minute. This feedback might include form, stroke rate, and efficiency of turns. Bambrick-Santoyo uses this as a metaphor to describe the school leader's role in improving instruction for students through the teachers. Instructional leaders can't improve student achievement by reading about the results of the state testing results in the newspaper. Instructional leaders can't change student outcomes just by reviewing internal testing data. They must be "at the pool" or in the classroom providing teachers valuable feedback during or immediately after a lesson.

The purpose of informal observations is to give teachers immediate and continuous written and verbal feedback on their instructional practices in specific areas. Providing teacher evaluations annually, semi-annually, or even quarterly may be too late to be effective. Informal observations focus intentionally on goals set in the teaching learning plan and assume that the area of focus will change frequently as the teacher improves.

Informal observations are unannounced, last for 20-30 minutes, and occur frequently throughout the year. Feedback is emailed to the teacher, and the teacher meets with the instructional leader biweekly to discuss progress.

The process goes as follows:

1. Conduct a 20 - 30 minute biweekly observation based on phase focus.
2. Inform the teacher immediately afterward via email (a teacher may respond and/or provide an explanation if needed).
3. Give informal verbal feedback biweekly for 20-30 minutes based on phase focus.

### Data Analysis & Coaching

The development of the data analysis and coaching used by Harvest Prep and Best Academy was highly influenced by two books: *Driven by Data* by Paul Bambrick-Santoyo and *The Data Coach's Guide to Improving Learning for All Students: Unleashing the Power of*

*Collaborative Inquiry* by Nancy Love, Katherine Stiles, Susan Murphy, and Kathryn DiRana[144] as well as by visits to high-performing charter schools from around the country, such as Roxbury Prep in Massachusetts. Materials from Achievement First's instructional framework were incorporated into the design.

The purpose of this section is to describe how teachers use data at Harvest Prep and Best Academy, and how the instructional leaders or coaches facilitate data meetings with both grade-level teams and individual teachers.

Teachers and administrators analyze data during three timeframes: daily, weekly, and every 6–8 weeks. Teachers meet with coaches weekly to review the data. Teachers have all three levels of assessment information available before they plan and teach lessons.

Daily analysis of student performance is done through exit slips, where students are asked to produce a product that aligns with the day's objective for that subject. Information from exit slips is used to plan future whole and small group instruction. The intent is to grade the exit slips the same day or for the next day, in order to inform the next day's lesson and instruction.

Weekly quizzes are given on Fridays to determine how students are progressing on the benchmarks. In grades K-4 quizzes are written for both mathematics and reading. For grades 5-8 each subject area teacher (mathematics, reading, science, and social studies) quizzes students on the benchmarks taught that week. All of these quizzes are common among all classes at each grade level. That data is then analyzed the following Friday afternoon.

Finally, a cumulative and formative assessment is given every 6–8 weeks (COMP) to assess how students have progressed over several benchmarks. Staff in grades 3-8 use a Scantron machine and bubble sheets to collect testing information; they use software called Prosper, which allows for multifaceted student-level reports aligned to the benchmarks. Full data days at the end of each COMP period are dedicated to data analysis, reteach week, and unit planning, as well as individual data meetings with administration and coaches. Teachers use a Cause and Verification form for every COMP assessment to determine root causes of performance. Student interventions are then planned on an on-going basis throughout the school year. A data manager works with teachers to (a) facilitate managing student-level data; (b) to create and maintain up-to-date student trackers; and (c) to use the Scantron machine. The data manager ensures that the technical pieces of the data process are in working order.

Coaching on data is done weekly during grade-level team meetings. Teaching and administrative staff analyze common quiz data using a tracker system that displays students' overall scores, student's individual scores, and scores by individual benchmark items. The tracker gives coaches information on how individual students are doing and what interventions they may need. It also gives teachers and administrators information on how any given class is doing on a given skill or concept. Individual data meetings occur every data day or five times a year. The individual data meeting goes over the data for each teacher's classroom. Teachers meet with their coach and go through an in-depth analysis of how their students are doing. They are expected to attend these weekly meetings and be prepared to discuss their quiz data.

Such meetings provide an additional layer of accountability, as teachers meet one-to-one with administrators and teacher leaders (instructional coaches) to ensure all students succeed in all areas assessed.

Every Friday is a half day of school for students. Data days, following COMP exams, are mapped out on the master school calendar as full days of professional development. The personnel responsible for administering and conducting these data days are administration, coaches, teacher leaders, and a full-time data manager.

At the beginning of every school year, new staff are trained on the data analysis system. Modeling of individual data meetings and training on data management is demonstrated by experienced teachers, coaches, and administrators to ensure that teachers understand what is expected of them and what the process looks like. All staff is required to read *Driven by Data* by Paul Bambrick-Santoyo as part of their individual professional development.

## Outer Ring 3 - School Structural, Operational, and Cultural Supports

### School Calendar, Bell to Bell, and Daily Schedule

The school calendar sets forth the total number of days the school plans to be open, the total number of hours it is in operation, and the total number of instructional hours that are available. In the Harvest Prep and Best Academy model, there are 195 school days, and nine hours per school day. This equates to 1,755 total hours the school is open for business. School starts at 8:00 a.m. and ends at 5:00 p.m. The longer day and year provide students with over 35% more time in school than the typical public school district (172 days of school for students with a 6.5-hour school day for a total of 1,118 hours). The additional 35% more time each year has a positive and cumulative academic effect on students. It gives them the ability to catch up academically if they are behind, and reduces the backslide that takes place for low-income children during the summertime learning gap. The longer school day and longer school year provide the school with the ability to individualize support using RTI to meet the needs of students and to give teachers more time to prepare lessons and analyze student data.

Given the additional amount of time that is available, Harvest Prep and Best Academy students have one additional year of educational advantage over the typical public school student for every three years that a student spends in this educational system. This means that a student, who starts in kindergarten at Harvest Prep or Best Academy and stays continuously enrolled through the 8th grade, will have a three-year academic advantage over the typical public school student.

### Daily Schedule

Academic work begins no later than 9:00 a.m. As mentioned above, there is a minimum of 100 minutes, with two class periods each, allocated for reading and math. Fifty minutes are allocated for social studies and another 50 minutes for science. There is also an intervention block of 50 minutes. The intervention block is used to help students who are behind catch up, but if the student is at grade level or ahead, the intervention block is used to move them ahead. Lastly, there is a teacher prep period of 50 minutes each day, when students are either in a physical education, computer science, music, or world language class.

The schools must devote at least 6.5 hours per day to academic instruction out of a nine hour school day, Monday through Thursday; on Fridays, five hours are allocated to academic instruction. The total number of hours per week for instruction is 31, and the average number of minutes devoted to instruction per day is 390.

The daily schedule is optimized for learning, because it gives students and teachers an extended period of time to devote to the core subjects of reading and math. They are core, not only because they are used as benchmarks for state comprehensive assessment testing, but because they have also been proven to be highly correlated with student success in other subject areas. The extended time also gives teachers the time for preparation and to differentiate instruction in the classroom.

## School Culture

The creation of, and emphasis on, school culture is an area that cannot be overstated. Schools must strive to create a culture of high expectations, a school ethos that expects academic success for all students. Positive school culture, including character development, will help build positive classroom culture and student engagement.

A school culture is created to accomplish at least four objectives. The first is to instill a growth mindset (effective effort) in our students. As explained in the section on the Belief Gap, having a growth mindset is critical to success, in particular in an educational setting where low-income students are continually subjected to challenges. Students with a fixed (innate ability) mindset avoid challenge. Students with the growth mindset see challenge as the natural process of learning.

The second objective of school culture is to create an expectation of high academic achievement. High-performing schools do not run from the problem by dumbing down the test or altering the standards. Far too many children of color believe that striving for high academic achievement is for White children or for "nerds." In too many schools and communities, high academic achievement is devalued. Harvest Prep and Best Academy create a culture in which every opportunity is taken to celebrate high academic achievement. This is done through regular award and recognition assemblies that take place throughout the school year after every grading period, during which academic achievement and growth are celebrated. Academic achievement is celebrated at parent and community gatherings during the school year when students perform the skills and abilities they have attained.

Incentives are also given to students for either high achievement or exceptional academic growth, such as additional computer time, additional gym time, etc. In educational parlance this is known as creating the "academic press"... [where] teachers, administrators, and students, are motivated by achievement-oriented goals, values, and norms.[145] It is "the extent to which the school is driven by a quest for academic excellence."[146]

The third objective of school culture is to create a safe and orderly environment where children feel protected and supported by adults and other students in the school building. Many children in low-income communities come from families and communities that are unsafe. They bring these fears to school. Teachers and administrators must be aware of the environments from which these students come and build an environment that allays these environmental concerns, which would otherwise impede student learning. It is difficult to learn in an environment that is chaotic and unsafe. Effective schools also have systems in place to protect and support teachers by ensuring that even adults interact and communicate to each other in a respectful manner. This includes how the teacher communicates with parents and how parents communicate with teachers.

Lastly, an effective school culture must build a system to cultivate student self-esteem using history and culture as a lever. African-American children, in particular, have been given a distorted image of themselves. All too often the image of young African-Americans is associated with drugs, gangs, and misogynistic rap music. It is imperative to address their psychological trauma. As studies conducted over the past 50 years have shown, such as the *Doll Study*, African-American children, not to mention children of other ethnic groups, associate blackness with being bad; "Black" is not someone with whom you would want to be associated. Even African immigrants who come from war-torn countries and refugee camps are warned to stay away from African-Americans and their negative culture and lifestyle of gangs, drugs, and crime. The consequence of this perpetual negative image of African-Americans has created a warped ("crooked room") self-image in African-American children. The solution to this problem is to give these students a clearer, more balanced, and positive picture of their history and culture. There are three ways in which school culture is shaped.

### Community Meetings

The first way in which school culture is shaped is by direct teaching. Harvest Prep and Best Academy use the biweekly community meetings to infuse culture throughout the student body. At least two days each week, there is a community meeting from 8:30 a.m. to 9:00 a.m. for all students. The importance of this community meeting cannot be overstated. It is used to build the school culture and to indoctrinate students to a belief system of high expectations and effective effort. Teachers and administrators use the word of the day, quote of the week, video lectures, and other teaching methods to instill the desired school culture.

### Classroom Culture

The second way in which school culture is shaped is in the classroom. Successful teaching can happen only when a teacher has created a positive classroom culture. In order to facilitate this process, the teacher needs to know what they want the students to be doing at all times. The teacher should use "what to do" statements when telling students exactly what is expected. It is important to create a classroom in which the teacher would like to spend her day. When a student's behavior needs to be corrected, the teacher should use positive framing to address the issue. By talking to students in a respectful way (which many students are not used to); by teaching students problem-solving strategies (which they can use instead of fighting); and by modeling the use of these strategies in the classroom, the teacher can address any issue with positive framing.

Teachable moments to reinforce character skills can also be successfully used by a great teacher. Students will value the things on which teachers place the most importance. Teachers and administrators must be conscious not to repeat or support negative stereotypes with their students. A teacher at Best Academy openly referred to his class of boys at a staff meeting as "a bunch of thugs." He was fired immediately. African-American children, and boys in particular, do not need such negative reinforcement; these types of comments have no place in an educational setting. To address these issues, teachers must first be aware of their own biases, and they must be culturally aware. Professional development time is spent making sure teachers and administrators are aware of the perceptions they bring to the classroom. They are also given professional development training about the culture and background of the students they are teaching.

## School-wide Culture

The third and final way in which school culture is created is through the creation of a school-wide culture. Before starting the first day of school, it is important to determine what kind of culture a school is striving for, both for students and teachers. For teachers and staff at Harvest Prep and Best Academy, a culture is created in which teachers instill students with a growth mindset. A teaching culture is created in which collaboration, hard work, resilience, and genuine interest in the health and welfare of the children is a priority. Staff must have a sense of urgency in educating students, and must have the ability to act on that sense of urgency.

The culture of the school starts with the vision of the staff and how they want the students to behave throughout the school day and in what areas of the building the behavior is expected. A detailed list of expectations of student behavior is generated for every area of the building. The following is a partial list of the different expectations throughout the day and in different areas of the building: classroom, hallways, entering the building, exiting the building, cafeteria, library, bathrooms, in assemblies, in groups, how we get students' attention, what we call students, how we discipline students, how students are rewarded and recognized, and what messages will be posted on classroom walls and in hallways in order to influence students. An example of this is an expectation of silent transitioning in the hallway. This makes transitions smooth, keeps students focused, and reduces discipline problems. It also respects the learning time of students who are still in the classroom.

Students are recognized based on the mission of the school as well as the things that the school believes are important. For instance, every Friday students are recognized for superior academic, social, and moral development. They are also recognized for homework completion. As teachers present these awards they explain to students why they're receiving them. These recognitions help to build the kind of culture sought in our students.

Harvest Prep and Best Academy use many different kinds of methods to instill the kind of values that the school wants to see in its students, for example, creeds, chants, song, stories, and metaphors. Here is an example of the Best Academy Creed:

Who's the best?

We are the best?

And we won't settle for less!

We are boys striving to become great men.

We are the best

Because we work hard at it!

We make no excuses.

We ensure that we are always prepared.

We will uplift each other.

We are our brother's keeper.

We are the best.

We will persevere.

We will be honest in our words

And honorable in our actions.

We will stand strong and proud.

We are the best.

We are determined to live up to our full potential.

We are creative leaders,

We will honor our past

And prepare for our future.

We give our best every day!

We are the best

We value education,

We are college bound,

We will respect our parents,

And honor our elders.

We will demonstrate positive behavior

In the community.

We are the best.

Not because we say it,

Because the best is what we do!

We are the best!

## Operations

We will not go into detail concerning school operations as it relates more to the business and administrative operations of a school; whereas, the focus of this book is teaching. It goes without saying that school operations have a direct impact on the academic side of the schoolhouse, especially if the operations are not aligned with the factors that impact student achievement. For example, transportation schedules must serve the daily schedule as well as the school calendar, which the school believes is optimum for student achievement. Transportation must be orderly and allow for minimal behavioral problems. They have an impact on school culture and, therefore, on student achievement.

Food service is also essential. The day starts with breakfast for all students. As research and science has proven, breakfast is the most important meal of the day. It is a well-known fact that many low-income children come to school without having eaten a nourishing breakfast. Just as a car cannot run without gas, a child cannot learn without having the necessary fuel to create the energy needed to learn.

Since many children at Harvest Prep and Best Academy are eligible for free and reduced lunches, getting a nutritious meal is absolutely essential. Students are eligible to receive breakfast, lunch, and snacks at the school.

## School Finance

"No money, no mission!" is a great summary of the relationship between school finances and the ability of a school to achieve its mission. School finance is a discipline unto itself. It is critical to get a great financial manager, whether a contractor or employee, to manage the school finances so that the school leader can manage the school. The following principles are used to manage the school's finances. First, the school funds are made available to schools to support the effective education of children. This is a very important principle because some schools focus on building a significant fund balance, even though their children are doing poorly. It would be a far better use of funds if they used the money to hire more effective teachers, or to hire a consultant with proven academic success to show them how to increase academic performance.

Schools must be able to obtain funding to supplement state support in order to recruit and maintain the best teachers and administrators, to provide professional development training, and to support student literacy through in-school, after school, and to fund extended school day and school year programming. As mentioned in the Acknowledgements section of this book, Harvest Prep and Best Academy have achieved much of their success due to the tremendous support received from philanthropic organizations. In addition to professional development and student literacy support, foundations have provided funding for the complete makeover of our schools' library and provided computer workstations for the children. They have provided food support for families, and have offered their professional employees to provide mentoring support to students. These actions have helped close the achievement gap.

## Bell to Bell

Bell to Bell is a term many schools use that describes the proper level of efficiency, effectiveness, management, and student engagement during a class period. From the bell that designates the start of class to the bell that designates the end of class, the teachers and students are doing everything possible to maximize learning.

Learning time is referred to as Bell to Bell in the Gap-Closing Framework. Many countries that lead the world in educational outcomes provide more learning time to their students. Learning time is one of the most powerful weapons used to close the achievement gap by high-performing schools. Locally Harvest Prep and Best Academy have closed the achievement gap primarily by leveraging time.

The most effective teachers maximize class time and leave nothing to chance. In many cases they are meeting and greeting their students at the door of their classroom and explaining to them the expectations to the students as they enter class. For instance, a greeting may go something like this: "Good morning scholars, it is wonderful to see you! We have a lot of work to do today, so we want to get started right away. You have exactly 20 seconds to place your homework from last night in the homework bin. As you walk into the classroom, put your coats and backpacks away. I want you sitting down right away. There's a Do Now on the board, and you have exactly three minutes to complete this exercise. If you complete the exercise earlier, then take out your reading book until everyone is done." The teacher will then shake every single student's hand before she crosses the threshold with a greeting such as "Good morning, Scholar (name of the student). Are you ready to learn today?"

Effective teachers anticipate anything that may waste time. They have sharpened pencils ready for children who may have forgotten theirs. They use signals for students that need to go to the bathroom, want water, or need a tissue. All of these signals are used to minimize disruptions in the classroom. Students are trained to sit up at all times and focus on or track the speaker.

We hope that this summary of the Gap-Closing Framework at Harvest Prep and Best Academy begins to give educational leaders and teachers an idea of the methods and practices that are used. As we know, having a playbook is one thing; having the leaders and players to execute it is quite another.

# 7

## 10 Best Practices of Gap-Closing Schools[147]

In the fall of 2010, the leaders of four of the five top gap-closing schools in the Twin Cities metropolitan area of Minnesota came together to talk about how they could pass on knowledge and understanding of their practices to other public school leaders and teachers. They met for six months to plan a symposium and workshop training session. As a part of that undertaking, they compared notes and came up with 18 best practices used among their schools. They determined that there were 10 best practices on which they all agreed. Since the purpose of this book is to show how to close the achievement gap, Chapter 7 presents the 10 best practices used by all four gap-closing schools.

### 1. A Coherent Instructional Philosophy

Success does not just happen. Schools that succeed want to succeed. They make it a point that they are going to succeed. Every staff member is aligned with the mission of success. As discussed earlier in this book, success is part of the Belief Gap, the Teaching Gap, and the Leadership Gap. Gap-closing schools understand that they live and die for student success. The phrase, "it isn't working," is enough to change policy. Experts and theoreticians may say it's supposed to work, but if that is not the case, then gap-closing schools change it to make it work, starting with the goal. They also have a very important understanding: student success is measurable. The teacher's or parent's claim that little Jane is the best must be backed by measurable evidence. Similarly, for gap-closing schools it's not enough to claim that they are doing right by the kids; data is needed to prove the results.

## 2. A Culture of High Expectation and High Achievement

Not only do gap-closing schools believe that all students can grow, they believe that every student must grow. It's not that they foster the belief that all students must perform the same; in gap-closing schools, the school accommodates whatever the student needs. However, they don't accommodate excuses. Whether for students or teachers, gap-closing schools distinguish between a legitimate need and an excuse. Needs are met; excuses are not tolerated.

In support of the belief that all students must grow, gap-closing schools make a point of highlighting student success. They bring out the band! They hang streamers and balloons! It's a big deal! They also bring in outsiders to show that *if this student did it, so can you*. It is an important part of creating the culture. For example, Harvest Prep and Best Academy have frequent award assemblies at which honor students are recognized and rewarded. They also hold parent and community events throughout the year to highlight student and school success. During the 2012-13 school year parent and community events were held and local radio, television, and print media announcements were made when Harvest Prep and Best Academy received the Futures Award from the Minnesota Business Partnership as the top two schools for closing the achievement gap; when Harvest Prep and Best Academy received recognition as Reward schools by the state of Minnesota Department of Education; and when Best Academy was nationally recognized as one of the top five schools by the Coalition of Schools for Educating Boys of Color (COSEBOC).

### 3. A Rigorous Curriculum

Gap-closing schools don't just "wing it." There has to be a rigorous curriculum. While research clearly demonstrates that the magic is not in the curriculum itself—what works for some schools, may not work for others—gap-closing schools use the curriculum as a plan. And while almost all gap-closing schools deviate from the plan, the deviations are planned and measured. Preparing and planning are critical to achieving the goal. Thus, in gap-closing schools, the curriculum is developed in advance and planned backwards to meet the state standards and benchmarks. The curriculum is what controls any deviation.

### 4. Data-Driven Teaching

Gap-closing schools live and die by the data. They push the data all the way down to the grass roots—where it belongs—to the teachers. The data does not belong in the principal's office or with a district assessment coordinator. It belongs to those who need it the most, who are most affected by it. Teachers must have access to the data, and they must be able to use it in a real-time setting on a daily and weekly basis. Even the students have access to the data. They have access to their scores and are taught, at their level, what that data means. Students can name their target. If little Johnny scored 176 and his target is 196, he knows what the target is. The whole school is oriented around getting the student to their target. Little Johnny buys into it. When little Johnny comes out of the test and has reached his target, he gets a high five! That is important to him!

And yet, schools can get overwhelmed with data. But what's important is not the quantity of the data, but its timeliness and usefulness. A teacher cannot wait two weeks while someone puts the data into an attractive presentation. Gap-closing schools use the summative, formative, and informal assessment data today!

### 5. Continuous Formative Assessments

Gap-closing schools use continuous formative assessments. Their purpose is to determine whether the teacher succeeded in delivering the benchmark and that the student mastered it. If not, then the school intervenes right away. The teacher may not be at fault—children have different learning styles and rates of progress, but the test suggests that a different style or approach may be needed. That's how continuous formative assessment is used; it is the hallmark of schools that close the gap.

### 6. Frequent Informal Observations

Gap-closing schools use frequent informal observations of their teachers and teacher assistants. The purpose is not to punish, but to evaluate and redirect the focus, attention, and workload, if necessary. School leaders must know what is not working and fix it. An effective school leader cannot wait until the state test results come in to say that the teacher does not get rehired. Informal assessments take place throughout the year to help the teacher succeed.

### 7. Targeted Student Support and Intervention

The formative assessment of the students, the informal assessment of the teachers, and targeted student support and interventions are all connected. When learning has not occurred, gap-closing schools calibrate the intervention to the source and level of the problem. If it's an individual student problem, the intervention is geared to that student. If it's a group of students, the intervention is geared to that group. If the entire class is having a problem, the intervention is geared to the entire class. At gap-closing schools, interventions do not wait, they occur within 24 hours, a week at most.

## 8. Reading and Writing Across the Curriculum

In gap-closing schools, language acquisition constitutes a massive gap. Children from economically and socially disadvantaged families enter school far behind in vocabulary compared to students from middle- and upper-income families. Consequently, reading and writing must be taught across all subjects. The science teacher is a reading and writing teacher, the social studies teacher is a reading and writing teacher, the gym teacher is a reading and writing teacher. In the *90/90/90 Study*, one of the distinguishing features of the high-performing schools was that students had to write in every course. Researchers have found that writing requires an advanced level of thinking and communication that teachers can easily evaluate to determine whether a student understands the subject matter.

Techniques and interventions used with English Language Learners (ELL) and special education students can be used across curriculum. Everybody understands ELL techniques, even if the students are not ELL students. Similarly, special education techniques can be used to intervene, even if the students are not special education students. Gap-closing schools do whatever it takes to succeed.

## 9. Teaching to the Whole Child

Gap-closing schools are often accused of "teaching to the test." But quite the opposite is true. Gap-closing schools teach to the whole child. The student cannot be reduced to her test score. Even though gap-closing schools live and die by the data, there are things about education that cannot be measured. Gap-closing schools understand that they must teach things like integrity; they care about unmeasurable things, such as a child's well-being and happiness. They strike a balance between the measureable and the unmeasurable.

### 10. Professional Development Training

All gap-closing schools require professional development training that is practitioner focused. Theory is not important; what matters is whether it works in the classroom on a Monday morning. In order for professional development to be effective, teachers must want help, and they must ask for it. It does no good to attend professional development training or seminars without engaging and having the desire to improve. As a part of professional development, teachers must not build artificial boundaries or fiefdoms, which inhibit assessment, feedback, and improvement.

# Conclusion

The following quote from Ronald R. Edmonds is the message that this book seeks to impart:

*How many effective schools would you have to see to be persuaded of the educability of all children? If your answer is more than one, then I submit that you have reasons of your own for preferring to believe that basic pupil performance derives from family background, instead of schools' response to family background.*

*...*

*We can, whenever and wherever we choose, successfully teach all children whose schooling is of interest to us. We already know more than we need to do that. Whether or not we do it must finally depend on how we feel about the fact that we haven't so far.*[148]

We hope you come away from reading this book believing that the education gap can and should be closed. This book offers the history, theory, and practice behind closing the gap with a cohort of children whose family background was given as the reason for their failure, but the founders of Harvest Prep and Best Academy did not accept that reason. They set out to demonstrate that in-school factors trump family background in defining the ability to educate children at the greatest risk of academic failure. Despite the fact that the students come from family backgrounds with the highest rate of single-parent, female head of households; the highest rates of unemployment; the highest rates of poverty; the highest rates of student and family mobility; and the highest rates of crime and incarceration, these schools have achieved outstanding success.

There are many different examples from around the country of highly successful school programs: the Harlem Children's Zone, KIPP (Knowledge is Power Program), Uncommon Schools Network, Yes Prep, and Achievement First. While styles and strategies may differ, the common threads of success were given as examples in the last chapter on the 10 Best Practices.

For policymakers and others interested in education, this is a story of success and an analysis of how it was achieved. We no longer have to ask the question of whether it can be done. Beginning in 1984 Ella and Eric Mahmoud had a vision that they should do something to address the educational disparities for children who are at the greatest risk for academic failure. They knew from their own family backgrounds and school histories that they had the ability to make a difference. The motivation to act came from the encouragement of those historians and elders who had imparted their knowledge and understanding of African-American history and culture, and taught them that education is the foundation for community development. From Dr. Amos Wilson, to Dr. Naim Akbar, to educator and historian Mahmoud El-Kati, each provided a model for moving forward. Little did the Mahmouds know that the preschool they incorporated in 1985 would grow into five schools, educating more than 1,000 students each year; and that in 2011 they would become what the superintendent of Minneapolis Public Schools described as "the highest performing public schools in Minnesota serving a high percentage of minority students."

As a society we know the social costs associated with the lack of an effective education. The term cradle-to-prison pipeline has its origin in the lack of effective education. Education, or more accurately the lack of education, is tied directly to juvenile and adult incarceration, unemployment, welfare, and poverty. More than 70% of the occupants of our prison system are functionally illiterate, and the cost of housing and caring for juvenile and adult prison inmates is five to ten times the cost of educating a child. As the Black abolitionist

Frederick Douglass stated more than 100 years ago, "It is easier to build strong children than it is to repair broken men," to which we might add: "And far less expensive."

Harvest Prep and Best Academy have demonstrated that they can take the same cohort of low-income and socially disadvantaged children that everyone else has destined for the societal scrap heap and turn them into high-achieving, productive contributors to society. Beginning with Eric Mahmoud's life-changing surgery in 2005, he set about demonstrating that it could be done. In 2008 Harvest Prep was considered the Best of the Worst. Employing his engineering background and applying attention to detail, he began to produce the prototype for academic success for low-income African-American children. Eric Mahmoud wanted to become the "Best of the Best".

Coincident with that mission, the leaders of Harvest Prep recognized that the achievement of their boys lagged substantially behind that of its girls. Consequently, a new strategy was put in place. Best Academy was created and specifically designed to address the unique educational needs of boys. Modeled after the successful teaching paradigm of the Harvest Prep co-ed program, Best Academy would close, and in fact, reverse the achievement gap for African-American boys within the space of three years, progressing from the 57th percentile in math to the 80th percentile, and from the 50th percentile in reading to the 85th percentile.

The groundbreaking "5 Gaps" analysis of the educational achievement gap, developed by Eric Mahmoud, gives educators, legislators, business leaders, social service agencies, and philanthropic organizations a framework for both understanding the cause and effect of the achievement gap and identifying effective solutions. Based on more than 25 years of study of successful programs from around the country, as well as on experience in education and business, Eric Mahmoud applied the "5 Gaps" analysis in fashioning a remedy to close the gap.

All that is needed now is for others to accept the premise that all children, regardless of background, have the ability to learn; and that it is incumbent upon us as leaders and educators to employ the proven solutions to make sure that it happens. Failure is not an option. Our very way of life depends on it!

# Endnotes

1.     Scores from the 2009 Programme for International Student Assessment released in 2010 showed 15-year-old students in the U.S. performing about average in reading and science, but below average in math.

2.     Associated Press. (2010, December 7). In ranking, U.S. students trail global leaders. USA Today. Retrieved from http://usatoday30.usatoday.com/news/education/2010-12-07-us-students-international-ranking_N.htm

3.     Jan. 2011, *The State of Minnesota Public Education*, a MINNCAN Research Report.

4.     From the Promise Neighborhood proposal of the Northside Achievement Zone, citing statistics from the Minneapolis Police Department, Social Explorer, City of Minneapolis, and Minneapolis Department of Health and Family Support.

5.     The Northside Achievement Zone (NAZ), a program in north Minneapolis, was patterned after the tremendously successful Harlem Children's Zone in Harlem, New York. A major focus of NAZ is to reduce the educational achievement gap for children in the zone. NAZ recently received a $28 million dollar Promise Neighborhood award from the federal Department of Education.

6.     Adi, H., Shahadah, A., Nehusi, A., (2005) Transatlantic Slave Trade.Retrieved from http://www.africanholocaust.net/Articles.

7.     Original small group of parents at Ella's daycare in 1986 included Bennice Young, who would later become a principal for Minneapolis Public Schools and Kim Ellison, who would become a Minneapolis school board member. Kim's husband, Keith, would become the first African-American congressman from the state of Minnesota and the first Muslim congressman in the history of the country.

8.     Madhututi, H., & Madhubuti, S. (1994). *African-centered education, its value, importance, and necessity in the development of Black children*. Chicago, IL., Third World Press.

9.     Wilson, A. N. (1978). *Developmental psychology of the Black child*. New York, N.Y., Africana Research Publications.

10.     Demographics of Philadelphia. (n.d.). *In Wikipedia*. Retrieved from http://en.wikipedia.org/wiki/Demographics_of_Philadelphia

11. Gurian, M. (2007). *The minds of boys: Saving our sons from falling behind in school and life*. San Francisco, CA., Jossey-Bass.

12. Kunjufu, J. (2005). *Keeping Black boys out of special education*. Chicago, IL., African-American Images.

13. Room to read. (n.d.) *In Wikipedia*. Retrieved from http://en.wikipedia.org/wiki/Room_to_Read. John Wood, founder and board co-chair, launched Room to Read in 1999 after a trek through Nepal, where he visited several local schools. He was amazed by the warmth and enthusiasm of the students and teachers, but also saddened by the shocking lack of resources. Driven to help, John quit his senior executive position with Microsoft and built a global team to work with rural villages to build sustainable solutions to their educational challenges.

14. Mike Mattos, principal of Pioneer Middle School in Tustin, California. Under his leadership, the school has had consistent outstanding student achievement. Based on standardized test scores, Pioneer ranks first among Orange County middle schools and in the top 1% of California middle schools. Matos was named the Orange County Middle School Administrator of the Year by the Association of California School Administrators.

15. "Got the people, but not the skills" (2011, October 26). *Minneapolis StarTribune*. Retrieved from http://www.startribune.com/opinion/editorials/132570618.html

16. ibid.

17. Servaas van der Berg is Professor of Economics at the University of Stellenbosch, South Africa, and holds the National Research Foundation's Research Chair in the Economics of Social Policy. His research and publications are mainly on income distribution and poverty, the economics of education, the economic role of social grants, and benefit incidence analysis. He has been extensively involved in policy research and advice for a wide range of institutions, including the World Bank and a large number of government and other organizations.

18. van der Berg, S., 2008, *Poverty and Education*, Paris and Brussels, International Academy of Education, International Institute for Educational Planning (UNESCO), citing Amartya Sen. Sen is an Indian economist and philosopher who was awarded the 1998 Nobel Prize in Economic Sciences for his contributions to welfare economics and social choice theory, and for his interest in the problems of society's poorest members. He helped to create the United Nations Human Development Index. Retrieved from https://en.wikipedia.org/wiki/Amartya_Sen

19. ibid.

20.  van der Berg, op. cit. Endnote 18.

21.  van der Berg, op. cit. Endnote 18.

22.  Roberts, L. (1998, October 14). *Illiteracy on the rise in America.* Retrieved from http://www.wsws.org/en/articles/1998/10/ill-o14.html

23.  ibid.

24.  Roberts, op. cit. Endnote 22.

25.  Kelly, L., and Egbert, A., 2011, *One Minneapolis: Community Indicators Report,* Minneapolis, MN., The Minneapolis Foundation.

26.  U.S. Government Printing Office, Superintendent of Documents. (1998), *The State of Literacy in American, Estimates at the Local, State and National Levels,* Washington, D.C.

27.  Kelly and Egbert, op. cit. Endnote 25.

28.  Carnevale, A. P., Rose, S. J., Cheah, B. (2011, August 5). *College payoff: Education, Occupations, Lifetime Earnings.* Washington, D.C., Georgetown University, Center on Education and the Workforce. Retrieved from http://cew.georgetown.edu/collegepayoff/

29.  Walmsley, R. (2009). *World Prison Population List* (8th ed.). International Centre for Prison Studies, London, School of Law, King's College.

30.  Greenberg, E., Dunleavy, E., Kutner, M., May 8, 2007, *Literacy Behind Bars: Results From the 2003 National Assessment of Adult Literacy Prison Survey,* National Center for Educational Statistics, Washington, D.C., U.S. Department of Education.

     Categories of literacy assessment - Below Basic indicates that an adult has no more than the most simple and concrete literacy skills. Basic indicates that an adult has the skills necessary to perform simple and everyday literacy activities. Intermediate indicates that an adult has the skills necessary to perform moderately challenging literacy activities. Proficient indicates that an adult has the skills necessary to perform more complex and challenging literacy activities.

31.  Drakeford, W., 2002, The impact of an intensive program to increase the literacy skills of youth confined to juvenile corrections, *Journal of Correctional Education,* Volume 53, Issue 4.

32.  Jacobs, E. M. & Steinberg, M. A. (2010, August). *Secondary teacher knowledge of reading instruction.* Tampa, FL., Juvenile Justice Education Institute & Southern Conference on Corrections.

33.    Enrico Moretti holds the Michael Peevey and Donald Vial Chair in Labor
       Economics at the University of California, Berkeley and is the author of *The
       New Geography of Jobs* (Houghton Mifflin Harcourt, 2012).

34.    Moretti, E. (2005). *Does education reduce participation in criminal activities?*
       Paper presented at the Equity Symposium, "The Social Costs of Inadequate
       Education," New York, Teachers' College, Columbia University. See more at
       http://www.centerforpubliceducation.org/Main-Menu/Staffingstudents/Keep-
       ing-kids-in-school-At-a-glance/Keeping-kids-in-school-
       References.html#sthash.XcRMM4rk.dpuf

35.    Smith, K. (2012, January 14). Bid for students now starts at crib. *Minneapolis
       StarTribune.*   Available   from   http://www.highbeam.com/doc/1G1-
       277299067.html

36.    According to Second Chance, Day on the Hill, the average cost of an adult
       prison sentence is calculated by multiplying the average length of stay, 605
       days (according to the Minnesota Department of Corrections' Fiscal Year
       2008 Report) by the per diem cost of incarceration in a Minnesota adult
       facility, $89.77 per day (according to the Minnesota Department of Correc-
       tions, Notable Statistics as of July 1, 2008). The juvenile cost was provided by
       the Minnesota Office of Juvenile Justice Programs. Retrieved from
       http://www.180degrees.org/pdf/SCD-postcard-5.pdf

37.    Runyon, R., (1996),*The roles of infrastructure and technology in delivering
       literacy services*, Library of the University of Nebraska, Omaha.

38.    Cortright, J. (2010, January). *The fiscal return on education; How educational
       attainment drives public finance in Oregon.* Retrieved from http://depts.wash-
       ington.edu/ uwcel/
       e3_obc/fiscal_return_on_education.pdf

39.    Shapiro, T. M., Meschede, & T., Sullivan, L. (2010, May). *Racial wealth gap
       increases fourfold* [Research and policy brief], Waltham, Institute on Assets
       and Social Policy, Heller School for Social Policy and Management at Brandeis
       University. Retrieved from http://www.insightcced.org/uploads/CRWG/IASP-
       Racial-Wealth-Gap-Brief-May2010.pdf

40.    Perry is the founder and principal of what U.S. News and World Report has
       cited as one of the top schools in the country, Capital Preparatory Magnet
       School in Hartford, Connecticut. Capital Prep has sent 100% of its predom-
       inantly low-income, minority, first generation high school graduates to four-
       year colleges every year since its first class graduated in 2006.

41.    Kelly and Egbert, op. cit. Endnote 25.

42.  See, for example, the 21st Century Foundation's Black Men & Boys Initiative; Project 2025 Network for Black Men & Boys; Kellogg Foundation's National Task Force on African-American Males; Open Society Foundation's Campaign for Black Male Achievement; Mitchell Kapor Foundation's Black Boys College Bound Initiative; ABFE's Black Men and Boys Initiative; Knight Foundation's Black Male Engagement; the Heinz Endowments African American Men and Boys Initiative.

43.  See, for example, the Report of the Task Force on the Education of Maryland's Black Males (March 2007); Task Force on the Condition of African American Men in Illinois (2009); Indiana Commission on the Social Status of Black Males (2009-2010); the Ohio Commission on African American Males (1989).

44.  James, M. C. (2010). Never quit: The complexities of promoting social and academic excellence at a single gender school for urban African American males. *Journal of African American Males in Education*, 1(3), 167-195.

45.  Mauer, M. & King, R. S. (2007, July). *Uneven justice: state rates of incarceration by race and ethnicity.*, Washington, D.C., Sentencing Project; Retrieved from http://www.sentencingproject.org/doc/publications/rd_stateratesofincbyrace-andethnicity.pdf

46.  Lyons, C. J. & Pettit, B. (2011). Compounded disadvantage: Race, incarceration, and wage growth. *Social Problems*, 58(2), 257-280.

47.  Top five reasons why teacher turnover is rising (2011, August 11). *Huffington Post*. Retrieved from http://www.huffingtonpost.com/2011/08/11/ top-5-reasons-why-teacher_n_924428.html

48.  Studt, D., and Smith, T., (2010), T*eacher Turnover in Charter Schools, National Center on School Choice*, Vanderbilt University, Nashville, Tennessee.

49.  Vaden-Kierman, N., Ialongo, N., Pearson, J. & Kellam, S. (1995). Household family structure and children's aggressive behavior: A longitudinal study of urban elementary school children. *Journal of Abnormal Child Psychology* 23 (5), 553–568.

50.  Sheline, J.L., Skipper, B.J., & Broadhead, W.E. (1994, April). Risk factors for violent behavior in elementary school boys: have you hugged your child today?*American Journal of Public Health*, 84(4), 661–663.

51.  Matlack, M. E., McGreevy, M.S. Mac, Jr., Rouse, R. E., Flatter, C., & Marcus, R. F. (1994). Family correlates of social skills deficits in incarcerated and non-incarcerated adolescents. *Adolescence* 29, 119-130.

52. Founded in 1996, the Gurian Institute is committed to helping boys and girls reach their full potential by providing professional development that increases student achievement, teacher effectiveness, and parent involvement.

53. 2011 Minnesota Comprehension Assessment (MCA) II.

54. Gladwell, M. (2008). *Outliers: The story of success.* New York, N.Y., Little, Brown & Company. See page 15.

55. Gladwell, ibid.

56. Reynolds, A. (2007, September 28). *Eight points on the achievement gap.* Presentation to the DFL Education Foundation.

57. Hart, B., Risley, T., 1995 (1st Ed.), *Meaningful differences in the everyday experience of young american children*, Baltimore, MD., Paul H. Brookes.

58. ibid.

59. Reynolds, A., Rolnick, A.,(2011), *Assessing the validity of Minnesota school readiness*, Minneapolis, MN., Human Capital Research Collaborative is a partnership between the University of Minnesota and the Federal Reserve Bank of Minneapolis Retrieved from http://humancapitalrc.org/mn_school_readiness_indicators.pdf .

60. ibid.

61. Other significant findings from the early childhood study conducted by the U.S. Department of Education were that average television watching between White and Black children showed a 38% difference (13 hours vs. 18 hours per week); there was a 30% difference between White and Black parents reading to their children (87% vs. 67%).

62. Mueller, Dan, (2005), *Tackling the achievement gap head on*, St. Paul, MN: Wilder Research.

63. ibid.

64. Mueller, op. cit. Endnote 62.

65. Wilder Research. (2008). *Draft: A collective plan for early childhood care and education in Minnesota.*, St. Paul, MN.

66. Dr. Carol Johnson is currently the superintendent of schools for Boston Public Schools; and, former superintendent of Minneapolis Public Schools.

67.  McREL is a private, 501 (c)(3) education research and development corpora-tion. Since 1966, when it was founded to turn knowledge about what works in education into practical guidance for educators, McREL has grown into an organization with more than 110 employees and a wide array of clients and contracts in nearly 50 states and around the world.

68.  Saphier, J., Haley-Speca, M.A. & Gower, R. (2008, 6th ed.) *The skillful teacher: Building your teaching skills*, Acton, MA: Research for Better Teaching. P. 52.

69.  Von Drehle, D. (2010, July 22). *The case against summer vacation.* New York, TIME Magazine. Retrieved from http://www.time.com/time/magazine/article/ 0,9171, 2005863,00.html

70.  Anderson, C.J.,(2011), *Why an opportunity gap results in the observed achieve-ment gap,* Retrieved from http://ucan-cja.blogspot.com/2011/12/why-oppor-tunity-gap -results-in-observed .html

71.  Holzman, M., (2010), *Yes We Can: The 2010 Schott 50 State Report on Black Males in Public Education,* New York, N.Y., The Schott Foundation Retrieved from: http://schottfoundation.org/news/8-17-2010/new-report-yes-we-can-public-schools-black-male-students.

72.  Saphier, Haley-Speca, & Gower, op. cit. Endnote 68.

73.  Berliner, D., (1990), *What's All the Fuss About Instructional Time*, Arizona State University, Retreived from http://www.timeandlearning.org/?q=time-learning -theory

74.  Prater, M.A., (1992), Increasing time on task in the classroom. *Intervention in School and Clinic*, 28, 22-27.

75.  Prater, M.A., (1992), Increasing time on task in the classroom. *Intervention in School and Clinic*, 28, 22-27.

76.  Saphier, Haley-Speca, & Gower, op. cit. Endnote 68.

77.  Reeves, D. (2000), *The 90/90/90 Schools: A Case Study, Accountability in action; a blueprint for learning organizations.* Englewood, Co., Advanced Learning Press.

78.  Minnesota Business Partnership and Itasca Project (2009). *Minnesota's future: World-class schools, world-class jobs.* St. Paul, Minnesota.

79.  ibid.

80. Education Trust, Inc. (2006). *Education watch Minnesota: Key education facts and figures. Achievement, attainment and opportunity from elementary school through college*. Washington, D.C.

81. Hassel, B., and Hassel, E., (2011), *Seizing the Opporunity at the Top: How the U.S. Can Reach Every Student with an Excellent Teacher*,Chapel Hill, N.C., Public Impact.

82. ibid.

83. Policy Studies Associates for the Center for Public Education, (2005), *Key Findings From Research on Teacher Quality and Student Achievement*, retrieved from www.centerforpubliceducation.org

84. Dufour, R., Dufour, R., Eacker, R., and Many T., (2010), *Learning by doing: a handbook for professional learning communities at work*, Solution Tree.

85. Mueller, op. cit. Endnote 62.

86. Mueller, op. cit. Endnote 62.

87. Education Trust, Inc.(2006) *Education watch Minnesota: Key education facts and figures; achievement, attainment and opportunity for elementary school through college*, Washington, D.C.

88. Minnesota Chamber of Commerce (2010). *Business plan for K-12 education reform*. St. Paul, MN.

89. Hassel and Hassel, op. cit. Endnote 81.

90. Policy Studies Associates for the Center for Public Education, *2005, Key Findings From Research on Teacher Quality and Student Achievement*, retrieved from www.centerforpubliceducation.org

91. Snipes, J. & Casserly, M. C. (2004). Urban School Systems and Education Reform: Key Lessons From a Case Study of Large Urban School Systems. *Journal of Education for Students Placed at Risk*, 9 (2), 127–141.

92. ibid.

93. Emarita, B., (2010), Minnesota early care and education action plan: High impact opportunities for action: Perspectives of cultural communities of color, Minneapolis, Millennium Group.

94. Minnesota Business Partnership and Itasca Project, op. cit. Endnote 78.

95. Minnesota Business Partnership and Itasca Project, op. cit. Endnote 78.

96. Reeves, D. (2000). *The 90/90/90 Schools: A Case Study.* In D. Reeves, Accountability in action: a blueprint for learning organizations (pp. 185–209). Englewood, CO: Advanced Learning Press.

97. ibid.

98. Minnesota Business Partnership and Itasca Project, op. cit. Endnote 78.

99. Mayberry, Cheryl, (2010). *Drivers of the racial achievement gap.* Minneapolis, MN: African-American Leadership Forum, Education Work Group.

100. ibid.

101. Kania, J., Kramer, M., (2011, Winter) Collective impact, Stanford, CA., Stanford Social Innovation Review, 9(1C) Retrieved from http://www.ssireview.org/articles/entry/collective_impact

102. National Governors Association, Council of Chief State School Officers, & Achieve, Inc. (2008). *Benchmark for success: Ensuring U.S. students receive a world class education.* Retrieved from http://www.achieve.org/publications

103. ibid.

104. Kania & Kramer, op. cit. Endnote 101.

105. Dr. Robert Jones is the president of State University of New York (SUNY) at Albany.

106. Minnesota Business Partnership and Itasca Project, op. cit. Endnote 78.

107. Minnesota Business Partnership and Itasca Project, op. cit. Endnote 78.

108. Stolle, L., Temperley, J., (2009), Improving School Leadership; The Toolkit; Organization for Economic Co-operation and Development, p. 17. Retrieved from http://www.oecd.org/edu/school/44339174.pdf; See also: Jacobson, S., Brooks, S., Giles, C., Johnson, L. and Ylimaki, R. (Dec.2004) Successful School Leadership in High Poverty Schools: An Examination of Three Urban Elementary Schools, Retrieved from http://gse.buffalo.edu/gsefiles/documents/alumni/Fall08_Commissioned_ Report_NYS_Ed_Dept.pdf

109. Woodson, C, (1977) *Mis-education of the Negro*, New York, N.Y: AMS Press, Inc.

110. Stevenson, H., (1994), *The learning gap: Why our schools are failing and what we can learn from Japanese and Chinese education*, New York, N.Y: Simon & Schuster.

111. Jefferson, T. (1784). Notes on the State of Virginia. Electronic Text Center, Charlottesville, VA., University of Virginia Library. Available from http://etext.virginia.edu/toc/ modeng/public/JefVirg.html; See also: www.historytools.org/sources/jefferson-Race.pdf

112. Davis, K. L. (Writer, Producer, & Director). (2005). *A girl like me* (Motion picture). United States: Reel Works Teen Filmmaking.

113. Greenwald, A. G., & Banaji, M. R. (1995). Implicit social cognition: Attitudes, self-esteem, and stereotypes. *Psychological Review,* 102, 4-27.

114. Harris-Perry, M., (2011), *Sister citizen: shame, stereotypes and Black women in America,* New Haven, CT. and London, Yale University Press.

115. Dr. Jeff Howard, founder and president of the Efficacy Institute, is a trained social psychologist, who has developed a comprehensive set of field-tested training programs, consulting services, and materials for adults and youth. He is founder of J. Howard and Associates, a corporate training and consulting firm and part of the Novations Group, Inc. Dr. Howard holds an A.B. from Harvard College and a Ph.D. in Social Psychology from Harvard University.

116. Noguera, P. (2003, July). The trouble with black boys: The role and influence of environmental and cultural factors on the academic performance of African American males. *Urban Education* 38, 431-459.

117. Pedro Noguera is the Peter L. Agnew Professor of Education at New York University. Dr. Noguera is a sociologist whose scholarship and research focuses on the ways in which schools are influenced by social and economic conditions, as well as by demographic trends in local, regional, and global contexts He is the executive director of the Metropolitan Center for Urban Education and the co-director of the Institute for the Study of Globalization and Education in Metropolitan Settings (IGEMS). From 2008 to 2011, he was an appointee of the Governor of New York to the State University of New York (SUNY) Board of Trustees.

118. Foster, K. M. (2004, December). Coming to terms: A discussion of John Ogbu's cultural-ecological theory of minority academic achievement. *Intercultural Education,* 15 (4), 369–384.

119. Ogbu, J. U. (Ed.). (2008). *Minority status, oppositional culture, & schooling.* New York, N.Y., Taylor & Francis Group.

120. ibid.

121. Interestingly, subsequent generations from these communities have taken on many of the negative traits and characteristics of low-income communities in the United States and no longer find themselves at the top of the educational ladder.

122. Ogbu, op. cit. Endnote 119.

123. Ogbu, op. cit. Endnote 119.

124. Dweck, C. S. (1999). *Self theories: Their role in motivation, personality, and development.* New York, N.Y., The Psychology Press.

125. Mueller, op. cit. Endnote 62.

126. Holzman, M. (2010). *Yes we can: The Schott 50-state report on public education and Black males 2010.* Cambridge, MA., Schott Foundation for Public Education.

127. ibid.

128. Markavitch, V. L. (2006, September). Learning for all: What does it take? [Powerpoint] Retrieved from www.michiganedusource.org/.../fc06/Learning-ForAll-Markavitch.ppt

129. Reeves, D. (2000). *The 90/90/90 Schools: A Case Study. In D. Reeves, Accountability in action: a blueprint for learning organizations* (pp. 185–209). Englewood, CO. Advanced Learning Press.

130. Holzman, op. cit. Endnote 126.

131. Holzman, op. cit. Endnote 126.

132. Kelly and Egbert, op. cit. Endnote 25.

133. Kelly and Egbert, op. cit. Endnote 25.

134. Mueller, op. cit. Endnote 62.

135. Snipes & Casserly, op. cit. Endnote 91.

136. Snipes & Casserly, op. cit. Endnote 91.

137. Snipes & Casserly, op. cit. Endnote 91.

138. Dufour, R. Dufour, R., Eaker, R., Many, T. (2006). *Learning by doing: a handbook for professional learning communities.* Bloomington, Indiana: Solution Tree Press.

139. Guides, forms, and samples of documents from the planning, teaching & re-teaching, assessments, and reflection can be found at http://ericmahmoud.com.

140. Achievement First is a network of public charter schools in New Haven, Bridgeport, and Hartford, Connecticut and Brooklyn, New York. It was incorporated in 2003 and serves over 7,000 students from low-income and ethnic minority backgrounds who have achieved outstanding results.

141. TAP was founded by Lowell Milken in 1999 to significantly improve teacher recruitment, retention, motivation, practices, and performance.

142  Madeline Cheek Hunter (1916–1994) was an American educator who developed a model for teaching and learning that was widely adopted by schools during the last quarter of the 20th century. She was named one of the hundred most influential women of the 20th century and one of the ten most influential in education by the Sierra Research Institute and the National Women's Hall of Fame.

143. Bambrick-Santoyo, P. (2010). *Driven by data: A practical guide to improve instruction.* San Francisco, CA: Jossey-Bass.

144. Love, N., Stile, K., Murphy, S., DiRana, K., 2008, *The data coach's guide to improving learning for all students: Unleashing the power of collaborative inquiry,* Thousand Oaks, CA., Corwin Press.

145. Shouse, R. C. (1996). Academic press and sense of community: conflict, congruence, and implications for student achievement. *Social Psychology of Education,* 1(1), 47-68.

146. Hoy, W. K., Sweetland, S. R., & Smith, P. A. (2002). Toward an organizational model of achievement in high schools: The significance of collective efficacy. *Educational Administration Quarterly,* 38, 77-93.

147. From a presentation by Asad Zaman on February 4, 2012, at the Gap-Closed! Results Achieved! School Leaders and Teachers Symposium and Workshop, St. Paul, Minnesota, sponsored by the African-American Leadership Forum, University of Minnesota, General Mills Foundation, and Minneapolis Public Schools. Asad Zaman is a policy fellow at the Minnesota 2020, a non-profit public policy think tank; and senior consultant for Designs for Learning consulting group, in the areas of education, organizational and   financial management.

148. Edmonds, R. (1979). Effective schools for the urban poor. *Educational Leadership,* 37 (2), 15–23. Edmonds was leader of the Effective Schools Movement in the 1980s.

149. Please note that throughout the book when comparing the differences between two percentages, the most common analysis is to subtract the two percentages to determine the percentage-point difference. The authors have chosen to analyze the differences between two percentages as a "percentage of the percentage". For example on page 57 the graph shows the difference between Harvest math 81% proficiency and the state math 62% proficiency in 2012 was a 19 percentile-point difference. The actual percentage difference is 31%. This conclusion is derived by subtracting 62% from 81% and then dividing by 62% ( (81-62)/62) = 30.6.

# Bibliography

Anderson, C. (2011, December 5). *Why an opportunity gap results in the observed achievement gap.* Retrieved July 22, 2013, from ucan-cja.blogspot.com:http://ucan-cja.blogspo.com/2011/12/why-opportunity-gap-results-in-observed.html

Bambrick-Santoyo, P. (2010). *Driven by data: A practical guide to improve instruction.* San Francisco: Jossey-Bass.

Berliner, D. (1990). *What's All the Fuss About Instructional Time.* Tempe: Arizona State University.

Carnavale, A. R. (2011, August 5). *College payoff: Education, occupations, lifetime earnings.* Retrieved July 22, 2013, from Georgetown.edu: htty://cew.georgetown.edu/collegepayoff

Center for Public Education. (2005). *Key Findings From Research on Teacher Quality and Student Achievement.* Washington, D.C.: Center for Public Education.

Cortright, J. (2010). The fiscal return on educaton; How education attainment drives public finance in Oregon. *Impressa Economics.*

Davis, K. (Director). (2005). *A girl like me* [Motion Picture].

Drakeford, W. (2002). The impact of an intensive program to increase the literacy skills of youth confined to juvenile corrections. *JCE,* Vol. 53, Issue 4.

Dufour, R. D. (2010). *Learning by doing: a handbook for professional learning communities at work.* Bloomington: Solution Tree.

Dweck, C. (1999). *Self theories: Their role in motivation, personality and development.* New York: The Psychology Press.

Edmonds, R. (1979). Effective schools for the urban poor. *Educational Leadership,* 37(2), 15-23.

Education Trust, Inc. (2006). *Education watch Minnesota: Key education facts and figures. Achievement, attainment and opportunity from elementary school through college.* Washington, D.C.: Education Trust, Inc.

Emarita, B. (2010). *Minnesota early care and education plan: High impact opportunities for action: Perspectives of cultural communities of color.* Minneapolis: Millennium Group.

Flavin, P. and Hartney, M. (2013). The political foundations of the Black-White education achievement gap, *American Politics Research.*

Foster, K. (2004). Coming to terms: A discussion of John Ogbu's cultural-ecological theory of minority academic achievement. *Intercultural Education,* 15 (4), 369-384.

Gerald, C. (2008). Benchmark for success: Ensuring U.S. students receive a world class education. Washington, D.C.: National Governors Association, Council of Chief State School Officers & Achieve, Inc.

Gladwell, M. (2008). *Outliers: The story of success.* New York: Little, Brown & Company.

Goodrich, T. (2013). *Black-white education achievement gap is worsened by unresponsive State policymakers, Baylor study shows.* Baylor                                    University. http://www.baylor.edu/mediacommunications/news.php?action=story&story=130932It

Greenwald, A. &. (1995). Implicit social cognition: Attitudes, self-esteem, and stereotypes. *Psychological Review,* 102, 4-27.

Gurian, M. (2007). *The minds of boys: Saving our sons from falling behind in school and life.* San Francisco: Jossey-Bass.

Hart, B. a. (1995 (1st Ed.)). *Meaningful differences in the everyday experience of young american children.* Baltimore: Paul H. Brookes Publishing.

Holzman, M. (2010). *Yes We Can: The 2010 Schott 50 Sate Report on Black Males in Public Education.* New York: Schott Foundation.

Hoy, W. S. (2002). Toward an organizational model of achievement in high schools: The significance of collective efficacy. *Educational Administration Quarterly*, 38, 77-93.

James, M. (2010). Never quit: The complexities of promoting social and academic excellence at a single gender school for urban African American males. *Journal of African American Males in Education*, 167-195.

Jefferson, T. (1784). Notes on the State of Virginia. Charlottesville: University of Virginia Library.

Kania, J. &. (2011, Winter). *Collective impact.* Stanford Social Innovation Review, 9(1).

Kelly, L., Egbert, A. (2011). *One Minneapolis: Community indicators report.* Minneapolis: The Minneapolis Foundation.

Kunjufu, J. (2005). *Keeping Black boys out of special education.* Chicago: African-American Images.

Lyons, C. &. (2011). Compounded disadvantage: Race, incarceration and wage growth. *Social Problems*, 257-280.

Madhubuti, H. &. (1994). *African-centered education, its value, importance, and necesity in the development of Black children.* Chicago: Third World Press.

Markavitch, V. (2006). *Learning for all: What does it take?* Oakland: Michigan Association of School Administrators (MASA).

Matlack, M. M. (1994). Family correlates of social skills deficits in incarcerated and non-incarcerated adolescents. *Adolescence*, 119-130.

Mauer, M. &. (2007). *Uneven justice: state rate of incarceration by race and ethnicity.* Washington, D.C.: The Sentencing Project.

Mayberry, C. (2010). *Drivers of the racial achievement gap.* Minneapolis: African-American Leadership Forum/Education Work Group.

Minnesota Business Partnership and Itasca Project. (2009). *Minnesota's future: World-class schools, world-class jobs.* St. Paul: Minnesota Business Partnership and Itasca Project.

Minnesota Chamber of Commerce. (2010). *Business Plan for K-12 Education Reform.* St. Paul: Minnesota Chamber of Commerce.

Moretti, E. (2005). *Does education reduce participation in criminal activities? The Social Costs of Inadequate Education.* New York: Teachers College, Columbia University.

Mueller, D. (2005). *Tackling the achievement gap head on.* St. Paul: Wilder Research.

Mueller, D. (2008). *A collective plan for early childhood care and education in Minnesota* (Draft). St. Paul: Wilder Research.

Noguera, P. (2003). The trouble with black boys: The role and influence of environmental and cultural factors on the academic performance of African-American male. *Urban Education,* 38, 431-459.

Ogbu, J. (2008). *Minority status, oppositional culture & schooling.* New York: Taylor & Francis Group.

Prater, M. (1992). Increasing time on task in the classroom. *Intervention in School and Clinic,* 22-27.

Reeves, D. (2000). *The 90/90/90 Schools: A Case Study, Accountability in action; a blueprint for learning organizations.* Englewood: Advanced Learning Press.

Reynolds, A. (2007). *Eight points on the achievement gap*; presentation to the DFL Education Foundation. Minneapolis: University of Minnesota.

Reynolds, A., Rolnick, A. (2011). *Assessing the validity of Minnesota school readiness indicators: Summary report.* Minneapolis: Human Capital Research Collaborative.

Roberts, L. (1998, October 14). *Illiteracy on the rise in America.* Retrieved July 22, 2013, from World Socialist Web Site: http://www.wsws.org/ en/articles/1998/10/ill-014.html

Runyon, R. (Undated). *The roles of infrastructure and technology in delivering literacy services.* Omaha: University of Nebraska, Omaha.

Saphier, J. H.-S. (2008 (6th ed.)). *The skillful teacher: Building your teaching skills. Acton: Research for Better Teaching.*

Shapiro, T. M. (2010). *Racial wealth gap increases fourfold. Waltham: Institute on Assets and Social Policy,* Brandeis University.

Sheline, J. S. (1994). Risk factors for violent behavior in elementary school boys: have you hugged your child today? *American Journal of Public Health,* 84(4), 661-663.

Shouse, R. (1996). Academic press and sense of community: conflict, congruence, and implication for student achievement. *Social Psychology of Education,* 1(1), 47-68.

Smith, K. (2012, January 14). *Bid for students now starts* at crib. Retrieved January 14, 2012, from www.highbeam.com: http://www.highbeam.com/ doc/1G1-277299067.html

Snipes, J. &. (2004). Urban School Systems and Education Reform: Key Lessons From a Case Study of Large Urban School Systems. *Journal of Education for Students Placed at Risk,* 127-141.

Stevenson, H. (1994). *The learning gap: Why our schools are failing and what we can learn from Japanese and Chinese education.* New York: Simon & Schuster.

Stolle, L. T. (2009). *Improving School Leadership; The Toolkit.* London: Organization for Economic Cooperation and Development.

Studt, D. a. (2010). *Teacher Turnover in Charter Schools*. Nashville: National Center on School Choice, Vanderbilt University.

Superintendent of Documents. (1998). *The State of Literacy in America, Estimates at the Local, State and National Levels*. Washington, D.C.: US. Government Printing Office.

Vaden-Kierman, N. I. (1995). Household family structure and children's aggressive behavior: A longitudinal study of urban elementary school children. *Journal of Abnormal Child Psychology*, 553-568.

van der Berg, S. (2008). *Poverty and Education*. Paris and Brussels: International Academy of Education, and International Institute for Educational Planning.

Von Drehle, D. (2010, July 22). The case against summer vacation. *TIME Magazine*, pp. 36-42.

Walmsley, R. (2009). *World Prison Population List (8th ed.)*. London: International Centre for Prison Studies.

Wilson, A. (1978). *Developmental psychology of the Black child*. New York: Africana Research Publications.

Woodson, C., (1977), *Mis-education of the Negro*, Washington, D.C., AMS Press, Inc.

Zaman, A. (2012). *Ten Best Practices of Gap-Closing Schools*. Minneapolis: African-American Leadership Forum.

# List of Figures

# Index

Eric Mahmoud is the President/CEO/Founder at Seed Academy & Harvest Preparatory School & a charter school leader & expert. Eric Mahmoud has more than 20 years of hands-on experience in educational administration. His commitment to academic excellence is reflected in his passionate pursuit of policies and programs that support teachers, empower parents, and inspire students. He believes, fundamentally, that all children deserve, and must receive, a high-quality education.

To access resources referenced in this book and/or to have Eric speak at your event, then please visit the website below.

# ericmahmoud.com

Also contact Eric Mahmoud at info@ericmahmoud.com or Jeffrey A. Hassan at (763) 391-6439.